International Politics of the Arctic

This book offers a wide-ranging account of the emerging issues of international politics in the Arctic, and the emerging geopolitical debates that surround the region.

In this thorough but accessible book covering environmental issues, the author examines the geopolitics of emerging land and resource disputes and the rise of both nationalist and pan-Arctic movements in the region. Whereas existing literature on the politics of the Arctic tends to focus either on the environment or on geopolitical interests, this book considers both of these themes in addition to the politics of the region's indigenous peoples and provides an overview on the emerging issues of international politics in the Arctic. The book makes full use of pedagogic features such as maps, diagrams, timelines, biographies and boxes highlighting key concepts and issues in order to make this an accessible book for both students and scholars alike.

This book will be of interest to students and scholars of International Relations, Arctic Politics, Environmental Politics and European Politics.

Peter Hough is Lecturer in International Relations at Middlesex University, UK.

Routledge Advances in International Relations and Global Politics

International Politics of the Arctic

Coming in from the cold

Peter Hough

Routledge
Taylor & Francis Group

LONDON AND NEW YORK

First published 2013
by Routledge
2 Park Square, Milton Park, Abingdon, Oxfordshire OX14 4RN

Simultaneously published in the USA and Canada
by Routledge
711 Third Avenue, New York, NY 10017

First issued in paperback 2014

Routledge is an imprint of the Taylor and Francis Group, an informa business

British Library Cataloguing in Publication Data
A catalogue record for this book is available from the British Library

Library of Congress Cataloging in Publication Data
International politics of the Arctic : coming in from the cold / Peter Hough, [editor].
    p. cm. – (Routledge advances in international relations and global politics)
    Includes bibliographical references and index.
    1. Geopolitics–Arctic regions. 2. Political geography–Arctic regions. 3. Arctic regions–International cooperation. 4. Arctic regions–International status. I. Hough, Peter, 1967-
    JC319.I62 2013
    320.1'209113–dc23
                            2012046301

ISBN 978-0-415-66928-3 (hbk)
ISBN 978-1-138-90921-2 (pbk)
ISBN 978-0-203-49664-0 (ebk)

Typeset in Times New Roman
by Taylor & Francis Books

To Dave Humphreys and Tunç Aybak
Two old sea dogs and good mates

Contents

Illustrations

Figures

Tables

Boxes

Acknowledgements

Many people helped make this vague and long-standing idea of mine become a reality. Dave Humphreys helped to formulate the proposal, gave specialist advice on the environmental chapter and supplied many useful materials along the way. Tunç Aybak also gave advice on geopolitical themes and passed on many useful articles and books to me, as well as offering general encouragement and support.

I must also say 'tak' to Gunhild Hoogensen and the staff at the University of Tromsø who facilitated my visit in 2008, which was a great experience and helped sow the seed for this book. Thanks, too, to the Economic and Social Research Council (ESRC)—particularly Richard Powell and Klaus Dodds—for facilitating and funding my attendance at two events on the seminar series *Knowledges, Resources and Legal Regimes: The New Geopolitics of the Polar Regions* in 2011. The papers presented there and the discussions that they prompted were invaluable in advancing my understanding, particularly in regards to the politics of the indigenous peoples of the Arctic. My thanks go also to Yossi Mekelberg for allowing me to present a paper showcasing my research towards this book at Regents College in 2012 and to David Parish and the attendant students who provided encouraging and helpful feedback.

In addition, I am hugely indebted to Aqqaluk Lynge for taking the time to write back to me with an extensive and highly informative letter which greatly enriched my understanding of the influence of the Inuit Circumpolar Council.

Last, but not least, thanks to Lisa, Daisy and Rosie for their patience and encouragement. Yes, I have now finished it!

1 The international political wilderness

Box 1.1 Martin Frobisher

Figure 1.1 Martin Frobisher

English adventurer Frobisher led three Arctic expeditions in the 1570s, backed by Queen Elizabeth, hoping to return with gold and charts for a new sea route over the north of Canada to cut the costs of trading with Asia. The expeditions failed to locate the 'Northwest Passage' and ran into trouble after running into local Inuit, having expected the area to be uninhabited. Frobisher's ships did, though, return with huge amounts of ore ready to be smelted into gold. However, the apparent riches were illusory with the rock turning out to contain only iron pyrites or 'fool's gold'.

Frobisher, nonetheless, went on to have a remarkable life, travelling to the West Indies with Francis Drake where he did strike gold and serving as a key commander in the legendary

> defeat of the Spanish Armada by the English fleet in 1588. An adventurer to the end he was persuaded out of retirement by Walter Raleigh to fight the Spanish again in 1594 but was mortally wounded in doing so.
>
> (Smith *et al.* 2009: 41–42; Bindoff 1982: 258)

Over 400 years later, the story of the Arctic is, in many ways, the same. Businesses and governments still pursue the possibilities offered by a Northwest Passage and prospect for new riches, whilst often forgetting that a local Inuit population have long inhabited the region and have a right to be consulted and involved in any such undertakings. This contemporary story of reconciling international and indigenous interests in the Arctic is told in this book.

Introduction

By means of introducing this contemporary story, this chapter will set the scene by examining what the Arctic actually is, how indigenous people and outside interests have come to manifest themselves in the region and how we can understand this in the context of International Relations (IR) theories rarely applied to this part of the world, traditionally viewed as on the margins of international political interest.

What is the Arctic?

The Arctic is an unusual region in many respects. It is a vast expanse of land, sea and ice spanning three continents and all time zones but ruled by remote control through capitals far to the south. Quite how vast the region is, how many people live there and which countries exercise sovereignty over it, though, is not easy to say, since there are several competing definitions of how far from the North Pole the Arctic actually extends.

Geographic

The Arctic can be defined geographically in reference to the Arctic Ocean and the lands that surround it, in the same way as it is possible to construct regions based on the Mediterranean, Black, Baltic seas and others. Under this rationale there are five Arctic states: Russia,

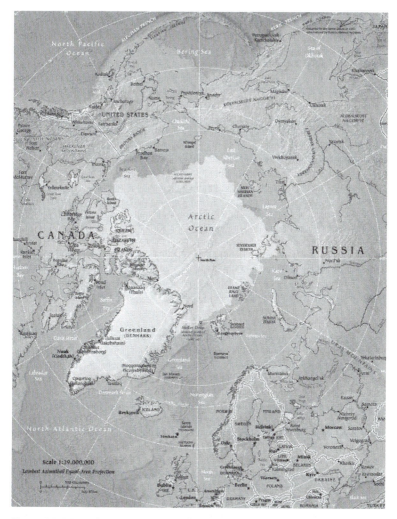

Figure 1.2 Map of the Arctic: a political projection
Source: Courtesy of the University of Texas Libraries, The University of Texas at Austin

Canada, Norway, Denmark (through its colony Greenland) and the United States. Unlike the aforementioned regions, though, the fact that most of the northern ocean is frozen over has limited the development of the same kind of international human community based on trade and the co-management of maritime resources. Despite some talk of an

'Arctic Mediterranean' in the emerging geopolitics literature of the 1940s, as it became apparent that the focus of power in the world was moving away from Western Europe (Stefansson 1943), the Cold War put paid to any prospect of this coming to pass with the two new superpowers, despite their proximity, seeing the region only in terms of strategic competition rather than economic cooperation. Traditional commercial links between Alaskan and Siberian Inuit across the Bering were even curtailed by the Soviets as an 'ice curtain' descended in the High North. The end of the Cold War and the retreat of the ice sheets has reawakened the 'Arctic Mediterranean' dream and the 'Arctic 5' (or 'A5') are now discussing how best to share the potential spoils once locked inaccessibly under the ice. International regions, even when defined on the basis of a geographical entity, are always socially as well as geographically constructed. The outer boundaries of an ocean are not always clear cut and the precise line of demarcation between the Arctic and Atlantic is debateable. How far inland the 'sense of region-ality' extends amongst settlements is also always a moot point. Iceland's exclusion by this definition may seem anomalous since it has the nearest sovereign capital city to the North Pole and strikes most people as a more Arctic-oriented country than the United States or Denmark. Icelanders certainly see it this way and have staunchly resisted literal, littoral definitions of the Arctic by the 'A5'.

Scientific

The best-known means of defining the Arctic is on the basis of including everything above the 66° 32 minutes north polar circle. This is a line of latitude demarking northern and southern zones of the Earth where, for at least one day per year, the sun does not set and does not rise. This has found favour because of its definitional preci-sion and is politically more inclusive, adding three more Arctic states into an 'A8': Iceland, Finland and Sweden. Iceland, in fact, only just makes it on this criterion as the Arctic Circle lies above its mainland but does bisect the tiny island of Grimsey off its northern coast. This understanding of the Arctic is the basis of the work and membership of the most important international political body in the region: the Arctic Council. A limitation of this definition, though, is that it has little climatological meaning which, to most people's eyes, is the most defining characteristic of the Arctic. The Arctic Circle runs south of boreal forests in Sweden and north of many treeless landscapes and polar bear habitats in Canada. Canadians, hence, generally favour an even more extensive definition of the Arctic.

Canadian

Canada has traditionally considered the lower 60° line of latitude, rather than the polar circle, to demark the Arctic. The 60th parallel does quite neatly divide Canada geographically and politically into its southern metropolitan federal states and three thinly populated northern 'territories'. This definition also has the neatness of mirroring the internationally acknowledged limits of Antarctica (since some of that continent protrudes north of the Antarctic Circle). However, this line also lacks climatological meaning outside of Antarctica and Canada. The 60° line applied to Europe would bring into the equation clearly temperate landscapes and would even make the UK an Arctic state, since it bisects the Shetlands.

Climatological #1: the tree line

A more visible and environmentally meaningful way to define the Arctic is to include everything north of the 'tree line'—a line north of which there are no high-growing trees or bushes. This demarcation has clarity since boreal forests (the *taiga*) thrive in a band around most of northern Europe, Asia and America, above which is the clearly contrasting *tundra* marked by permafrost and only dwarf forms of vegetation. A drawback of this means of defining the Arctic is that it cannot, of course, be applied to the Ocean and seas. Iceland, again, misses out on the basis of this definition in spite of its glaciers.

Climatological #2: the 10°C July isotherm

A way of delimiting the Arctic on a climatological basis that can be applied on land or sea is to use a line based on long-term mean temperature. The 10°C isotherm in July, the warmest month, is similar to the tree line, thus producing a more comprehensive environmental region. However, there are some variations and most of Iceland is included in this construction of the Arctic.

Countries, hence, tend to prefer regional definitions that favour themselves. According to the Icelandic parliament:

> The Arctic region should therefore be regarded as a single vast area in an ecological, political, economic and security-related sense, but not in a narrow geographical sense with the Arctic Circle, tree line or a temperature of 10 degrees centigrade in July as a reference point.

(Althingi 2011)

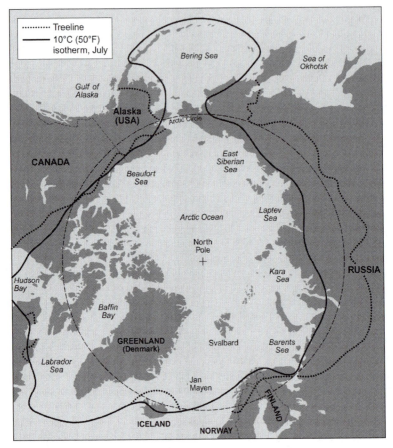

Figure 1.3 Map of rival definitions of the Arctic

An objective, definitive understanding of what is and is not the Arctic does not exist but contemporary practice has tended to settle on the scientific definition and this study will follow suit, even though demarking a region on the basis of daylight has no real political or geographical meaning.

Beyond seeking objectively to determine the extent of the Arctic, an ontological inquiry into the region must also take into account its subjective meaning to the wider world in political and popular imagination. The romantic 'other worldliness' of the Arctic contributes to making it of interest even to those with no stake in the region. It is the home of Father Christmas to many of the world's children, the lair of reputedly the world's most deadly creature and the backdrop to many of history's bravest feats of exploration. With the onset of climate change, we now see the region also cast as the symbol of global catastrophe with the imagery of melting glaciers, homeless polar bears and the loss of a winter wonderland consciously employed to popularize the cause. Hence, the Arctic emerged as the unlikely backdrop to British party politics in 2006 with Prime Minister-to-be David Cameron seeking to prove his green credentials by staging publicity shots dog-sledding over a glacier in Spitsbergen.

Such symbolic meaning is coming to be better appreciated in the study of international politics as the discipline matures beyond assuming that all decision making boils down to an objective cost-benefit analysis. 'Who gets what' is certainly an important dimension of the international politics of the Arctic but the symbolic and subjective meaning attached to the region also enters into political calculations. For Russians and Canadians in particular, the frozen north is part of their national identity. For much of the world, the visible decline of this great wilderness epitomizes wider human failings and a dysfunctional international political system, and has served to heighten interest in a previously neglected end of the Earth.

A history of the Arctic in international affairs

Four broad 'families' of indigenous people comprise the pre-modern population of the region: Paleo-Siberian, Eskimo/Aleut, the Sami and the Yakut. Paleo-Siberian peoples are believed to have inhabited the Russian Arctic as far back as 5,000 BC and their descendants, including the Nenets, Komi, Chukchi and others, still reside there alongside Russian settlers today. The Eskimo and Aleut, who form a second major indigenous ethnic grouping, are believed to have migrated from Siberia across the Bering to North America between 2,000 BC and 4,000 BC, where they reside today alongside US and Canadian settlers. The Eskimo are subdivided into two ethnic groups—the Inuit and Yupik—who separated around 2,000 years ago (Encyclopaedia Britannica 2005). In Canada and Greenland, the term Eskimo has come to be seen as passé and superseded by the use of Inuit, but the two labels are not synonymous since the non-Inuit Yupik are found in Alaska and eastern Siberia. The Sami, the first settlers in Scandinavia, are Uralic peoples (and, hence, related to Finns and Magyars), and the Yakut are Turkic, descended from people who migrated north from Central Asia in the Middle Ages.

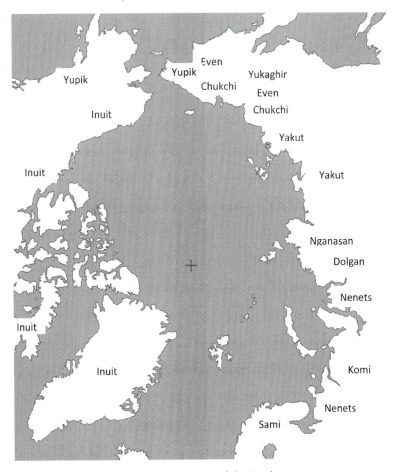

Figure 1.4 Map of the indigenous peoples of the Arctic

Arctic exploration from outside of the region declined from the 17th to 19th centuries, after Baffin's expeditions of 1615 and 1616, like Frobisher's, seemed to confirm that a Northwest Passage was a myth. Proof of the existence of the Northwest Passage was not confirmed until the separate expeditions of Franklin and McClure in the mid-19th century but, since this also helped establish that this sea route was frozen over, outside economic interest subsided. However, an international presence in the Arctic continued through a combination of the nationalist glory of discovery and international cooperation to advance the burgeoning science of meteorology. Roald Amundsen preceded his conquest of the South Pole with the first transit of the Northwest Passage in 1905, whilst, in between, a race for the North Pole was won (although disputed by some) by the American Robert Peary in 1909.

Sovereign claims over the lands of the Arctic have evolved since the time of Frobisher but have not always been strongly asserted until relatively recently.

Canada

The British laid claim to the Canadian Arctic archipelago and northern mainland from the 16th century in the wake of Frobisher's 'discovery' of Frobisher Bay on Baffin Island. However, in effect, they left the area to the Inuit he had encountered on his voyages.

United States

As befits vulgar stereotyping, the United States bought their way into Arctic politics with the purchase of Alaska from Tsarist Russia for US$7.2 million in 1867. There was no obvious return on this investment until around a century later, when the state became a useful hub in the US standoff with its former landlords and, particularly, when oil was then struck in 1968.

Denmark

A Nordic presence on Greenland can be dated back to the Icelandic Viking Erik the Red who established a settlement in the 10th century. Links between this settler community and Norwegian traders and missionaries led to Greenland being formally colonized by Norway in 1261. The Vikings later left, leaving the giant island to the Inuit, but it nonetheless came to be claimed as a colony of Denmark in the 18th century as they had taken over Norway and come to establish trading and religious links there.

Norway

The Spitsbergen archipelago has no indigenous population, but, after its location by Dutch explorer Willem Barentsz in 1596, it was visited by other of his countrymen along with British, Danish, French, Basque, Norwegian and German seamen on hunting and whaling missions through the 17th century. With whale and seal numbers depleted, such missions declined by the 19th century and, with international scientific cooperation beginning to flourish, Spitsbergen became a classic case in international law of *terra nullius* (land belonging to no one). However, the discovery of coal in the early 20th century and the independence of Norway (from Sweden) transformed the status of the islands, with the Norwegians and Swedes, along with Germany, Russia and the United States all wishing to be involved in some sort of international governance in order to protect emerging economic interests. A conference to flesh out such an arrangement was set for 1914 but was cancelled due to the outbreak of the First World War. The Great War worked in Norway's favour by effectively removing the defeated Germany and revolting Russia from the equation when they requested the right to assume sovereignty at the 1919 Paris Peace Conference. A Commission was established to examine this proposal, culminating in the 1920 Treaty Concerning the Archipelago of Spitsbergen, which came into force in 1925.

The Spitsbergen Treaty confirmed Norwegian sovereignty but with significant limitations on the exercise of this authority in a unique piece of international legislation. Citizens of any state party to the treaty are entitled to reside on the islands and not be discriminated against by the Norwegian government. The Norwegian government in their administration are also not allowed to profit from taxation, resulting in a break-even rate of income tax of around 8%. Neither Norway, nor any of the other parties, is permitted to militarize the islands. Despite their marginalization compared to the situation in 1914, Russia and Germany later became parties to the treaty, with Norway recognizing the USSR as a quid pro quo. With coal supplies becoming less profitable, most non-Norwegian mining operations pulled out of Spitsbergen in the 1910s and 1920s. Most notably, the Norwegian government had purchased 'Longyear City', set up by Boston businessman Longyear in 1906, from the Americans. The 'Norwegianization' of the islands was also reflected in them being re-branded from their Dutch title to the Norse 'Svalbard', with Spitsbergen now applied to the main island. To much of the outside world, though, Spitsbergen remains the name of the whole archipelago.

During the Second World War the British took responsibility for evacuating the islands, employing a 'scorched earth policy' to limit German interest, despite Norwegian opposition. Consequently, the Germans' presence on Spitsbergen was limited to manning weather stations, the last of which kept reporting right up until Berlin's surrender in May 1945, only to be left stranded by the hasty Nazi retreat from Norway. It was not until September 1945 that the team were discovered and rescued by Norwegian forces, prompting what was, technically, the last surrender by German forces to the Allies some four months after the war had ended (Umbreit 2009: 37).

Coal mining on Spitsbergen resumed after the war despite the depletion of the mineral, as for the Norwegians it represented their only domestic supply of the fuel, and for the Russians it presented an opportunity to retain a foothold in 'the West' in the new political landscape of the Cold War. The USSR, with troops stationed in Finnmark at the close of the war, had requested of the Norwegian government that they enter into a bilateral condominium over the whole archipelago or split it between them, with Moscow acquiring Bear Island. Neither option was taken up by Oslo, leading to a strange 'cross-curtain' co-existence during the Cold War with a Russian presence maintained around the settlement of Barentsberg, complete with a statue of Lenin, existing as an enclave on otherwise distinctly Norwegian territory. Today a small Russian/Ukrainian community remains on Spitsbergen but the population (of just under 3,000) has become more international, with scientists of many of the states party to the 1920 treaty manning numerous stations. There is also a burgeoning tourist trade, in spite of a century of poorly regulated mining having turned sections of pristine wilderness into a 'rustbelt industrial heritage park' (Anderson 2009: 122).

The island of Jan Mayen is unambiguously Norwegian sovereign territory. Although he was not the first to visit the island, Jan Mayen was named after the Dutch mariner Jan May, who visited there in 1614 prompting the establishment of a whaling base (Umbreit 2009: 218). The island was then deserted for over two centuries, after the whale stocks had been exhausted, before becoming an important hub for polar exploration and scientific cooperation in the late 19th century after it was used as a base for an Austro-Hungarian research station during the 1882–83 first International Polar Year. Norway annexed the island in 1929, after having established a weather station eight years earlier, and this was not officially contested despite some previous Danish assertions of interest (Umbreit 2009: 218–19). Jan Mayen was, in fact, the only Norwegian land not occupied by Germany—with a small garrison of Norwegian troops stationed at the weather station from 1941 resisting several Nazi attacks and downing two planes. The United States also set up a radio station on Jan Mayen during the Second World War. Between 1959 and 1960, the Americans then constructed an air strip and new radio station in the context of the Cold War, all done in secret since Norway had joined the North Atlantic Treaty Organization (NATO) with an undertaking not to permit US troops on their territory so as not to antagonize the Soviets. The radio and weather stations remain today but there is no indigenous or permanent population. The island is administered by the county of Nordland with authority delegated to the station commander of the Norwegian Defence Communication Service (CIA 2012). Tourism has not flourished as much as might be expected on this spectacular volcanic island due to the absence of cheap flights and ferry services.

Russia

The Soviets' initial exclusion from the Spitsbergen treaty prompted the young country to assert their sovereignty over Franz Joseph Land, Novaya Zemelya, New Siberian Islands and the remaining parts of Siberia that are today part of the Russian Federation. In a decree of 1926, the Soviet Union annexed all lands lying between the eastern and western extremities of their mainland and the North Pole according to the 'Sector Theory'. There was little legal basis to this annexation, given that sector theory has never been recognized as legitimate beyond the handful of countries for which it is convenient, and these lands had never been systematically inhabited and, as such, were *terra nullius*. Norway had a claim to Franz Joseph Land and Fascist Italy even made a spurious case for sovereignty in 1928, on the basis that the Austro-Hungarian Weyprecht and Von Peyer expedition that discovered the islands in 1873 set out from Trieste, but, in effect, nothing was really done to prevent this northwards Soviet thrust (Umbreit 2009: 196–98). Post-revolutionary Russia was not viewed as a threat by the Western powers in the way that it had been in the 19th century and would be again a couple of decades later, and these lands were also amongst the most obscure and inhospitable in the world.

Hence, Moscow's Arctic outposts effectively became cut off from the rest of the world from the 1930s to the 1990s and left to Soviet scientists, seamen and nuclear weapons. The Germans set up a weather station on Franz Joseph Land's Alexandra Land during the Second World War but had to abandon it after some of the unit died from contracting trichinosis from eating raw polar bear meat unsuited to the non-Inuit diet (Umbreit 2009: 198). During the Cold War, Franz Joseph Land was visited only by a few scientists from fellow socialist countries and also France, following their withdrawal from the military structure of NATO. Owing to its closer proximity to the mainland, the Russians had charted and hunted on Novaya Zemlya as far back as the 11th century but stepped up sovereign assertions in the 19th century, when Western European interests in a navigable route through the 'Northeast Passage' intensified. A few hundred Nenets were relocated in 1877 to ward off Norwegian claims, only for their descendants to be removed again in the 1950s when the islands became an important military and, in particular, nuclear testing site (Zeeberg 2001: 106–7). Since the 1990s, some tourism and scientific cooperation has developed but this is still limited due to the costs and some continuing Russian reticence. Franz Joseph Land's bases, for example, were closed to tourists between 1999 and 2002 (Umbreit 2009: 200). The New Siberian Islands and northern mainland outposts of Siberia, owing to their location, have never been within the realistic strategic interests of Western powers, although some local nationalist movements did resist the 1926 Soviet annexation.

Despite being under sovereign control by the 20th century, the Arctic region only sporadically featured in high politics and its native population was often left to its own devices. Even during the Cold War, the Arctic became a superpower backyard but something of a backwater, not featuring too prominently in diplomatic calculations other than in terms of its value as the shortest route for the firing of intercontinental ballistic missiles. Hence Russians and Norwegians co-existed on Svalbard and the USSR and United States cooperated in a landmark conservation regime—the 1973 Polar Bear Treaty—unimaginable at the time anywhere else in the world. Thus, the High North became the backdrop to the end of the Cold War with Mikhail Gorbachev choosing Reykjavik and Murmansk as the venues to offer olive branches to the West in 1986 and 1987, initiating regional cooperative ventures still evolving today. This new 'Age of the Arctic' (Young 1985) seemed to mirror the optimism of the wider new world order marked by greater international cooperation and a peace dividend able to be deployed on previously marginalized issues like environmental change, human rights and development. The prospect of climate change finally revealing the energy and mineral riches and a readily navigable Northwest (and Northeast) Passage that had attracted 16th-century kingdoms, though, has led many to speculate that the Arctic's coming in from the cold will, instead, see it become a new stage for imperial rivalry and a nationalist resource scramble.

The Arctic and International Relations theory

The Arctic is emerging as a region with political significance but predicting how this will affect it depends on your assumptions about International Relations. The four best-established schools of thought in the discipline are introduced below and will be referred to as the different themes of Arctic politics are analysed in subsequent chapters.

Realism

The Realists are the conservative traditionalists in International Relations who see the political world as being relatively simple and predictable. The Realist world is dominated by sovereign states pursuing their own self-interest (the 'national interest'), with international organizations and treaties serving as no more than vehicles for their convenience. Assuming base human motives of self-serving greed, these states are expected and advised to maximize their own power in order to survive in a competitive state system. Order in such an anarchic world can only come from a balance of power between the most powerful states being respected by them and the less powerful. Most Realist thought has metamorphosed into neo-Realism, which sees the world as less chaotic than the classical Realists, with some order additionally coming from a 'society of states' cooperating for their mutual convenience. For Realists of all shades, however, international relations is characterized by states pursuing their own interests.

Realists thus expect the emerging international politics of the Arctic to be marked by increased rivalry between the most powerful Arctic states ('the A5') seeking to advance their national interests by acquiring the new spoils.

Liberalism

Liberal thinking in International Relations opposes Realism both normatively and ontologically. In line with Liberal philosophy, IR Liberals consider cooperation, rather than conflict, to be the human instinct and both prescribe and predict the advancement of international organizations and international law beyond mutual state interest. IR Liberals also argue that the political world as seen by Realists is too simplistic and reason that international organizations and other 'non-state actors' (such as pressure groups and multinational corporations) increasingly rival sovereign states as the determinants of international political events.

Liberals thus can envisage a cooperative and pluralistic politics emerging in the Arctic with the states of the region working together to their mutual advantage through the Arctic Council and relying on international law to regulate any disputes that do occur. This perspective can also readily imagine non-governmental voices, such as the representatives of the region's indigenous peoples and international scientists, finding expression in the evolving political arrangements.

Marxism

A third school of IR thought comes from a variety of approaches which have adapted the key tenets of Marxist philosophy and economics to the study of world politics. In spite of the obvious decline of Marxism as an ideology of government in recent decades, it is an approach that many consider to have more pertinence than ever in terms of explaining the wider political and economic world. The IR Marxist view of the political world is focused not on the motivations of states or non-state actors, but of wider transnational classes: a global bourgeoisie and proletariat. IR Marxists are 'Structuralists', contending that events in the political world are dictated by the economic structure of the capitalist world in which the global bourgeoisie systematically accumulate wealth at the expense of the proletariat. This is not as straightforward as the wealthy states of the Global North dominating those of the Global South. Elites in the Global South (such as oil or diamond exporters) benefit from such accumulation and the working class in the Global North are amongst the exploited. This is a pattern that is assumed will persist as long as we inhabit a capitalist world in which profits are pursued at someone's expense.

For Marxists, then, the Arctic's entrance into more mainstream International Relations will inevitably see the region suffer the fate of imperial and neo-imperial peripheries and be exploited by the pursuit of profit by global business and political elites.

Social Constructivism

A fourth paradigm of International Relations has evolved since the 1980s through dissatisfaction with the explanatory powers of the three main perspectives. Social Constructivism, though, is not about opposing the other world views as much as building on them to produce a more complete understanding of International Relations. Social Constructivist writers often have Realist, Liberal or Marxist instincts but reason that these only take them so far in fully conceptualizing the political world. Social Constructivists contend that international affairs cannot always be explained rationally by a selfish Realist, cooperative Liberal or economically determinist Marxist model. In this view, human behaviour is not always predictable. Instead, it is reasoned that we act in the way we do sometimes because we believe in it or simply like the action we are taking, rather than to advance any material interests. In the same way, it is argued that states' foreign policies—and the policies of non-state actors—can be determined by ideas and cultural factors as much as the pursuit of power and wealth.

Hence a Social Constructivist take on the emerging politics of the Arctic would not necessarily dispute any of the aforementioned theoretical visions of the future, but contend that this cannot represent the whole picture. Concepts like sovereignty, globalization and security in a region like the Arctic are subjective social constructs and hence likely to be interpreted and responded to differently by different actors.

The next chapter begins the process of understanding the International Relations of the Arctic by examining the prospects of it, becoming an arena for new nationalist rivalries, in line with Realist assumptions.

2 Imperialism
The last great territorial scramble?

Introduction

Box 2.1 One small step for a robot ...

Figure 2.1 The Russian submarine North Pole landing

In 2007, the Arctic was uncharacteristically thrust to the fore-front of the world's media when a robot from a Russian submarine placed a national flag on the exact seafloor location of the North Pole for the first time in history in a symbolic act of conquest both retro and futurist. The Russophobic response of Western media and politicians to this stunt was also reminiscent of yesteryear fears provoked by 'the Bear' and seemed to many to be the likely precursor to a new, modern, high-tech geopolitical struggle between East and West. Canadian Foreign Minister Peter MacKay epitomized Western irritation at the Russian initiative by stating, 'You can't go around the world and just plant flags and say "we're claiming this territory".' However, the governments of Canada and fellow Arctic littoral states Denmark and Norway have been busy in recent years claiming extra territory, albeit in a less extravagant fashion. The melting of the Arctic ice sheets has opened up new possibilities for navigation, fishing and, most particularly, the exploitation of underground resources once thought too costly to extract.

This chapter explores this apparent new 'gold' rush and land grab in the last wild frontier that is the Arctic.

Box 2.2 Chilingarov and MacKay

Figure 2.2 Artur Chilingarov *Figure 2.3* Peter MacKay

Artur Chilingarov is an ethnic Armenian Russian explorer, writer and politician. He has been a member of the Duma since 1993 representing Nenets Autonomous Okrug as a member of Vladimir Putin's United Russia party. He led the 2007 North Pole submarine expedition for which he was awarded the honour of 'Hero of the Russian Federation', to add to his 'Hero of the Soviet Union' title earned in 1986 when he led a salvage operation after his ship was trapped in ice on an Antarctic expedition.

Peter MacKay became Canadian foreign minister under the Stephen Harper administration that swept to power in 2006 partly on the ticket of a more assertive Arctic policy after the two parties they led merged into a single Conservative Party. Harper and MacKay closely aligned themselves to the United States in relation to Iraq, Afghanistan and the Israel/Palestine dispute, but on the Arctic they were not afraid to confront their southern neighbour in asserting their country's sovereign claims. Despite being switched to defence minister by Harper in 2007, MacKay has remained a prominent and colourful political and media figure, married to a former 'Miss Canada' and touted by some as a future prime minister.

Frozen assets: the geopolitics of Arctic resources

At around the same time that the Russian robot was at the North Pole, the US Geological Society was carrying out a 'Survey of Undiscovered Oil and Gas in the Arctic', the results of which further kindled geopolitical interest in the region. The much-quoted survey estimated that the Arctic contained 22% of the world's undiscovered fossil fuels: 13% of oil and 30% of gas. This is in addition to proven reserves currently being extracted near the northern coasts of Alaska, Canada and Russia, amounting to 10% of the world's known remainder (USGS 2008) (see Table 2.1).

The US geological survey, carried out in conjunction with fellow geologists from Canada, Denmark, Greenland, Norway and Russia, divided the whole area north of the Arctic Circle into 33 geologically defined regions. Some 90% of the unclaimed hydrocarbons lie in eight fields identified in the map in Figure 2.4; 84% of all the undiscovered deposits are off shore.

Of these eight regions, three—Laptev, Yenisey-Khalana and West Siberia—lie exclusively within Russian sovereign jurisdiction. The Alaskan sea region is under US jurisdiction, whilst Denmark has sovereignty over the East Greenland region, although economic authority is now devolved to Greenland itself. The East Barents region is politically divided between Norway and Russia; Amerasia between Canada and the United States, and West Greenland/East Canada between the two named countries. All of these eight regions contain a

Table 2.1 Estimated oil and gas deposits in the Arctic

	Oil (billion barrels)	Liquefied gas (billion barrels)	Natural gas (trillion cubic feet)	Total (billion barrels equivalent)
Undiscovered	90	44.0	1,669	412
Known	40	8.5	1,100	240

Source: (USGS 2008)

Figure 2.4 Map of oil and gas reserves in the Arctic

range of fuels but West Siberia has by far the largest proportion of remaining gas and Alaska most of the oil. Containing estimated smaller amounts of hydrocarbons, but politically significant, are two huge regions spanning the North Pole area—Lomonosov-Makarov and the Eurasia Basin—much of which lies outside of the 200-mile exclusive economic zones (EEZ) of any Arctic states and therefore outside of any current sovereign authority.

Arctic oil is nothing new, of course. Commercial oil activity began in Canada's Northwest Territories in 1920, closely followed by ventures on the Kenai Peninsula in Alaska and Komi and Nenets regions of Siberia. The 1968 oil discovery at North Slope, Alaska, was a landmark breakthrough and this site has already produced 11 billion barrels of oil/gas since that date. At around the same time, the Soviet

Union made several new major gas discoveries in West Siberia and the Russians have been the world's biggest producer and exporter of that energy source since then. Off-coast drilling in the USSR, United States and Canada and also Norway (in the Barents Sea) then began to develop from the 1980s.

The oil multinational corporations (MNCs) 'supermajors' and state-owned energy companies have gradually moved further afield to explore these new options as Alaskan, Russian and Norwegian reserves have peaked. In 2011, after a barren decade, the Norwegian state-controlled Statoil, in conjunction with private domestic firms Eni Norway and Petoro, discovered 150–250 million barrels of oil on the Skrugard Prospect in the southern Barents Sea. BP have been active for several years in the Canadian Beaufort Sea and the US government in 2011 finally gave the go ahead for Shell to explore the Alaskan part of that sea, having restricted this for several years for environmental reasons. In the Russian Arctic Ocean, Western MNCs appear to have been falling over themselves to secure access to new oil and gas fields in cooperation with the state-owned groups. In 2011, the French-based giant TOTAL bought a substantial stake in Novatek to develop the Yamal liquefied natural gas (LNG) field, whilst United States-based Exxon-Mobil quickly stepped in to form a strategic partnership with Rosneft to look for oil in the Kara Sea, when a similar deal with BP was scuppered by domestic opposition. Prominent amongst newcomers on the bloc have been UK-based Cairn Energy, which was quick to negotiate the rights with the Greenlandic government to establish four new rigs in the Baffin Sea.

Going over the top: new sea routes

An added source of geopolitical interest in the Arctic being ushered in with the retreating ice is the potential realization of the long-lost dream of navigation through the seas of the region, abandoned over a century ago when it was found that the legendary Northwest Passage was frozen all year long. In 2007, this route opened up for the first time in living memory and there are now seven distinct routes via the Canadian archipelago that are open to maritime vessels other than icebreakers and submarines for a limited period in the summer, which will lengthen over time. A Northeast Passage, known to Russians as the Northern Sea Route, is also now opening up over that country's vast northern seaboard (see Figure 2.5).

The Northwest Passage takes 3,850 km off sea journeys between New York and Shanghai (currently quickest via the Panama Canal)

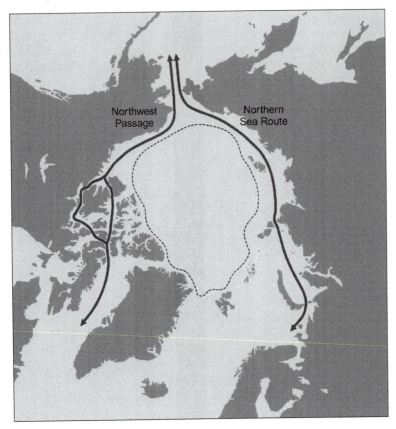

Figure 2.5 Map of the Northwest Passage and Northern Sea Route

and the Northeast Passage cuts sailing between London and Yokohama by 7,359 km (currently quickest via the Suez Canal)[1] (Christensen 2009: 2). In 2010, a ship belonging to the giant Russian mining firm Norilsk Nickel completed a trip from Dudinka in Krasnoyarsk Krai to Shanghai through the Northern Sea Route, 18,000 km in 41 days, less than half the time and distance of the conventional route via Suez.

High North, high politics

The combined effects of the Russian robot and the US Geological Survey prompted some shrill and bellicose reactions in the Western media and academia. A 2008 article in *Jane's Intelligence Review*, widely cited in the UK popular press, reasoned that Russia's recent war against Georgia and the general high stakes could see them and possibly other Arctic states 'make pre-emptive military strikes' to secure resources in advance of the United Nations Convention on the Law of the Sea (UNCLOS) adjudication of 2020 (Galeotti 2008: 11). Similarly, another widely cited article by a former US Coast Guard Officer in the conservative journal *Foreign Affairs* warned of 'armed brinkmanship' due to the anarchic nature of the emerging Arctic political landscape. 'Decisions about how to manage this rapidly changing region will likely be made within a diplomatic vacuum unless the United States steps forward to lead the international community toward a multilateral solution' (Borgerson 2008: 73). Across a range of publications, Cold War stereotyping came out of cold storage with a special edition of the *Eurasian Review of Geopolitics* on 'The Polar Game' similarly declaring that: 'Russia's decision to take an aggressive stand in the polar area has left the US, Canada and the Nordic countries little choice but to forge a cooperative High North strategy and invite other friendly countries, such as Great Britain, to help build a Western presence in the Arctic' (Cohen 2008: 36).

Seemingly supporting such reactions was a notable reassertion of energy security interests in a series of foreign policy statements and initiatives by the Arctic states in the late 2000s.

Russia

Whilst, as discussed in Chapter 1, the Soviet Union's acquisition of its northern and eastern hinterlands was legally ambiguous, taming and exploiting this wilderness represented a longstanding Russian ambition able to be acted upon with the unprecedented and unsurpassed industrialization and authoritarianism that marked Stalin's era. The Arctic became the backdrop to the purges with its Gulags holding many of that era's political prisoners. The 1933 construction of the Belomorkanal (White Sea Canal), linking the Baltic to the Arctic, claimed the lives of at least 25,000 penal workers (Emmerson 2010: 57–58). In 1937, in scenes similar to Chilingarov's expedition 70 years later, a Soviet plane became the first to land at the North Pole, symbolizing their claim to the land, sea and ice between here and their northern coastline. From the 1950s, the Soviet Arctic also became a key arena for nuclear weapons testing and deployment.

The Arctic later became a testing ground for a diametrically opposing phase of Soviet foreign policy in the 1980s when Mikhail Gorbachev made overtures of de-militarization and environmental cooperation in the region as part of his strategy of accommodation with the West.

After that, the Arctic became more marginal in Russian interests under the decentralized but Moscow/St Petersburg-focused administration of Boris Yeltsin, only to be revived in importance under Putin's centralization and drive for energy security. Chilingarov's mission thus appeared to symbolize Russia's renewed preparedness to assert itself in its own backyard after the humiliations of Western incursions into their Slavic periphery through North Atlantic Treaty Organization (NATO) expansion and the 1999 war with Yugoslavia. Although the North Pole robot was a private rather than a government mission, a subtext was that Moscow was at the time asserting that the Lomonosov submarine ridge, upon which the North Pole lies, was part of its continental shelf. This contention and the importance attached to the Arctic was articulated in a 2009 strategic document.

Box 2.3 Fundamentals of Russian state policy in the Arctic up to 2020 and beyond

- Define continental shelf claim
- Establish military and coastguard group to protect interests
- The Arctic would become 'the country's top strategic resource base by 2020'

(Russian Government 2009)

Canada

The Canadian government's withering response to the Chilingarov mission can be seen in the context of its own assertiveness in terms of claiming continental shelf high into the Arctic and holding on to what it already believes itself to own. A 'use it or lose it' attitude to its northern fringe has long informed Canadian policy and, in the early Cold War, manifested itself in the controversial relocation of Inuit communities northwards into uninhabited regions. In the post-Cold War era, the Canadians have asserted themselves more against their southern neighbour and close ally, with near-universal domestic backing for resisting US claims that the seas of the Northwest Passage are international rather than internal waters. In December 2004, the Canadian House of Commons voted, with none against and only one abstention, to rename the Northwest Passage the 'Canadian Northwest Passage'. The Arctic then became a key plank of Harper's successful nationalistic election campaign of 2006 and in his first week as prime minister he became embroiled in a row with the US ambassador to Canada over the legal status of the Northwest Passage. An annual military patrol of the Arctic region known as Operation Nunaliuut ('This Land is Ours') is now well established. Such a stance is supported by public opinion, with an extensive poll of the Arctic nations carried out by a Canadian university in 2011 finding Canadians to be 'least open to negotiation and compromise' and 'least open to cooperation' and to 'rate the Americans on the same level as Russians in terms of comfort levels' (CCGSS 2011: vii).

Box 2.4 *Comprehensive Northern Strategy: Our North, Our Heritage, Our Future,* **2009**

- Exercise Arctic sovereignty
- Social and economic development
- Environmental protection
- 'The North is central to the Canadian national identity'

(Canadian Government 2009)

USA

US Arctic policy over recent decades has been far less demonstrative than either the Russians or Canadians. They are not really part of any scramble for the Arctic other than wanting to resist the others scrambling for it and keep things largely as they are. The Arctic has, though, periodically been seen in the context of US vital national interests. Alaska had never featured much in US thinking since its 19th-century purchase, an act generally regarded as a folly. After the Second World War, though, the Truman Doctrine found expression in the north, with its strategic location between the new superpowers resulting in its being spoken of as a geopolitical 'new heartland'. 'If there is a third world war ... its strategic center will be the North Pole' (Murphy 1947: 61). Whilst at the time the United States was far ahead of the USSR in military power terms, there was a concern that they were behind them in this potentially vital arena. Hence, the United States reverted to 19th-century type and made an offer to Copenhagen to buy Greenland in 1946. The offer was rejected by the Danes but, nonetheless, they effectively ceded military control of the island to the United States, recognizing that, as was the case against Germany in the Second World

War, only the United States could secure them against the USSR. The United States similarly took over the defence of Iceland during the Cold War, as it had done in the preceding global struggle.

American interest in the Arctic was very much Cold War realpolitik and hence lessened in the 1990s. Whereas for the Russians and Canadians an Arctic presence is important for their national identities as well as national interests, it has tended to be purely viewed in terms of the latter for the United States. Energy interests and a desire to focus Congress on the potential offered by the Arctic prompted the George W. Bush Administration to release a Homeland Security Directive for the region in one of its last acts in the White House.

Box 2.5 *Homeland Security Directive on Arctic Regional Policy*, **2009**

- Energy security
- Freedom of the seas
- Military mobility in the region
- Keep the Arctic Council informal
- No 'Arctic Treaty'
- Ratify UNCLOS
- National interest should be pursued whether independently or collaboratively
- 'Assert a more active and influential national presence to protect its Arctic interests'

(US Government 2009)

The fact that the United States to date is still not a party to UNCLOS (United Nations Conference on the Law of the Sea) provides a classic example of 'bureaucratic politics' in foreign policy favoured by Liberal analysts over the 'rational actor' model of the Realists. The government has not been able to implement a self-identified national interest due to internal politicking. Presidents Bush and Barack Obama, Secretary of State Hillary Clinton and the US Navy have all promoted ratification, as did the Executive, Pentagon and energy industrialists at the outset of the legal instrument in 1973, but a group of isolationist senators have continually blocked this through fear of US sovereignty being compromised by becoming accountable to the International Tribunal for the Law of the Sea. In 2004, the Bush government secured Danish agreement for the Thule radar station to be revamped from its Cold War Distance Early Warning function to become part of the Missile Defence programme and carried out the 'Northern Edge' 12-day military exercise in the region in 2008. However, in many other respects, US military interests in the Arctic, unlike the rest of the Arctic 8, have lessened, as epitomized by the closure of their Keflavik base in Iceland in 2006.

Norway

The Arctic for the Norwegians has the intrinsic value that it has for Russians and Canadians beyond the instrumental value as a source of energy or military security that characterizes the US attitude. Due to the country's location, though, Oslo has always been more multilateralist and sensitive to Russian interests than Ottawa.

Box 2.6 *High North Strategy*, **2006**

- Environmental protection
- Sustainable development of resources
- Rights of indigenous peoples
- Develop transport
- Cooperation with Russia

(Norway Government 2006)

The themes of the *High North Strategy* were reaffirmed three years later in the 2009 *New Building Blocks in the North* report and that year also saw an apparent statement of intent when the government moved the national military headquarters from Jalta near Stavanger to Reitan, near Bodo in the north.

Denmark

Perhaps influenced by the fact that their days as an Arctic power may be numbered as Greenland edges nearer to full independence, Danish Arctic strategy has intensified in recent years. Hence, the *Strategy for Activities in the Arctic Area 2008* was followed up by a new, revamped strategy document just three years later. In between, in 2009, the Folketing voted to authorize the establishment of an Arctic military command and task force by 2014. Foreign Minister Per Stig Möller was also the architect of the 2008 Ilulissat Conference which appeared to sidestep Sweden, Finland and the European Union (EU) in heralding a new, more exclusive 'Arctic 5' ('A5') club, discussed in Chapter 5.

Box 2.7 *Strategy for the Arctic 2011–2020*

- Peaceful cooperation based on UNCLOS
- Maritime safety
- Sustainable development and resource extraction
- Climate change and biodiversity
- Rights of indigenous peoples
- Arctic and Nordic cooperation
- 'Arctic 5 is an essential complementary regional forum for the coastal states of the Arctic' (p.49)

(Governments of Denmark, Faeroes and Greenland 2011)

Finland

The assent of the Arctic 5 has seen the Nordic trio of Finland, Sweden and Iceland respond to the threat of marginalization by releasing their first strategic foreign policy documents on the Arctic, all of which stress the centrality of the Arctic Council in regional governance and advance a role for the EU in the emerging political landscape. The Finns, as the most Europhile Nordic state, have been particularly keen to develop a role for Brussels in the High North. An Arctic EU Information Centre has been established at Rovaniemi and the EU's Northern Dimension foreign policy strategy was launched in 2007 as an initiative of the Finnish government during their presidency. In 2010, Helsinki set up an Advisory Board on Arctic Affairs as a prelude for the release of a strategy document systematically articulating their position for the first time.

Box 2.8 *Finland's Strategy for the Arctic Region*, **2010**

- Environmental protection
- Research to aid Finnish exports in the region
- Develop northern transport routes

- Promote the role of indigenous peoples
- '[E]mphasize the Arctic Council as the primary cooperation forum on Arctic matters' (p.54)
- Make government funding for Arctic activities simpler
- 'Finland considers that it is important that the EU develops its own Arctic policy' (p.52)

(Finland Government 2010)

Iceland

Iceland felt most isolated by the Ilulissat Summit as it came two years after another watershed marginalization, this time in the military sphere, when the United States closed their Keflavik base. The defence pact of 1951 is still intact and Iceland still enjoys the guarantees of being a NATO member, but the withdrawal has still left many in the country feeling vulnerable. This vulnerability heightened with the banking collapse that accompanied the 2008 onset of global recession, which soured relations with the UK and the Netherlands (where many citizens had invested in these banks) and complicated an application to join the EU. Hence, Reykjavik has become creative in seeking allies including looking east to build relations with the Russians and Chinese. In building such bridges, President Olafur Grimson has noted the help given by China in comparison to the economic hostility of some Europeans and their security abandonment by the United States (Blonden 2012: 123).

Box 2.9 *Parliamentary Resolution on Iceland's Arctic Policy*, 2011

- Securing Iceland's position as a coastal state within the Arctic region
- Resolve conflicts via UNCLOS
- More cooperation with Faeroe Islands and Greenland
- Environmental protection and cooperation
- Resist the militarization of the Arctic
- '[F]urther efforts that may undermine the Arctic Council and Iceland's interests in the region must be resisted'

(Althingi 2011)

Sweden

The Swedes have also come to see the need to develop a more explicit Arctic strategy reinforcing the importance of the Arctic Council. The Swedish government had not formulated any official Arctic foreign policy strategy documents prior to 2011 when Foreign Minister Carl Bildt announced to the Riksdagen that such a publication would be released later in the year.

Box 2.10 *Sweden's Strategy for the Arctic Region,* **2011**

- Environmental sustainability
- Respect for the culture of indigenous people
- A 'more active' Arctic Council, which 'could reduce the need for the coastal states to drive forward issues in the Arctic Five format' (p.22)

(Sweden Government 2011)

Other actors

The EU has developed a northern position through its three Arctic member states and wider fears of a Russian and even Canadian carve-up, although, as illustrated earlier, this is less enthusiastically endorsed by the Danes with one foot in this camp and the other in the 'A5'. A European Parliament resolution of 2008 prompted the European Commission to release a communication in October initiating a new branch of the Common Foreign and Security Policy.

Box 2.11 *The European Union and the Arctic Region,* **2008**

- The EU is intrinsically linked to the Arctic and needs to respond on issues related to the region in a coordinated manner
- Protect the environment and exploit resources in a sustainable manner
- Improve multilateral governance
- Right of passage in newly opened shipping routes

- '[N]ot support arrangements which exclude any of the Arctic EU member state or Arctic EEA [European Economic Area], EFTA [European Free Trade Association] countries'

  (EU 2008)

European Parliament resolutions have been similar but more assertive, including a 2009 vote calling for an 'Antarctic-style' International Treaty for the Arctic. The EU has also attended the Arctic Council on an ad hoc basis and has since sought to acquire permanent observer status.

NATO held its first major Arctic seminar at Reykjavik in January 2009. The introductory speech by Secretary-General Jaap de Hoop Scheller at the event stated that 'NATO provides a forum where four of the Arctic coastal states can inform, discuss and share any concerns that they have', and also stressed that the NATO-Russian Council provides a possible vehicle for all five. As such, it is possible to conceive that NATO could become a more significant intergovernmental player than the EU, despite the much stronger advocacy for the latter in some quarters. A NATO Arctic presence was trumpeted in a 2012 'Cold Response' military exercise in northern Norway.

China has had a steadily growing presence in Arctic affairs over the last 30 years. Regular Chinese polar expeditions have been organized since the 1980s and the country has an established presence on Spitsbergen. China also possesses the world's biggest non-nuclear icebreaker, the *Xue Long* (snow dragon), and has growing interests in commercial shipping and securing new energy supplies. There have been no official proclamations from Beijing on the Arctic and a foreign minister in 2009 stated that 'China does not have an Arctic strategy' (Jacobson 2010: 9). Nonetheless, it seems safe to assume that free access through the two polar sea routes would be viewed as being in Chinese national interests and a Canadian/Russian/Danish extended continental shelf carve-up be seen as counter to them. Statements on the Chinese government website support this (China 2010). In a curious geopolitical twist, this could be viewed as placing the Chinese alongside the EU and United States in an Arctic 'great game'.

In spite of a lack of official statements, Beijing has, nonetheless, intensified diplomatic activity in the northern latitudes in recent years. China has the biggest embassy in Reykjavik and the seemingly mundane matter of the Icelandic premier's 2007 visit to Beijing was made into a lavish affair by the hosts (Blonden 2012: 128). In 2008, China supported Iceland's campaign to gain a seat on the UN Security Council and they have made some significant economic investments in the country including the controversial purchase of a 300 sq. km tract of wilderness in the northeast by the tycoon Huang Nubo. In 2012, Wen Jiaboa then made the first visit by a premier to Iceland in 40 years as part of a North European tour which also took in Sweden. Beijing have also courted the support of Sweden and Norway for gaining permanent observer status in the Arctic Council, at which they have previously observed in an ad hoc capacity.

Non-Nordic North European states have also begun to formulate foreign policy strategies for the Arctic independently of the EU. In 2010, the UK, Germany, Netherlands and Poland initiated meetings of the Northern Dimension Group of Defence Ministers, linking these four with the Nordic and Baltic states. In 2012, an embryonic British strategy emerged when the Foreign and Commonwealth Office produced a statement for a parliamentary committee on the government's objectives in the region, which was echoed on their website. The statement highlighted British commitment to the Arctic Council (at which they have had observer status from the start) and the 'Polar Code' of safety standards produced by the International Maritime Organization (based in London) and environmental protection in words that, overall, were reminiscent of the Swedish government strategy (FCO 2012). In practice, in recent years, the British have positioned themselves close to Norway, most notably in supporting them over their claim to control the 200-mile EEZ around Svalbard, which is opposed by most states. Germany has also courted an Arctic suitor in the form of Iceland with all major political parties declaring their support for their EU application in spite of a general national antipathy to further enlargement (Blonden 2012: 123). A huge growth in German exports to China also makes the Northern Sea Route of particular importance (ibid.: 118).

The North Asian shipping powers of Japan and South Korea also have an evolving role in Arctic diplomacy. South Korea, owing to their particular expertise in constructing icebreakers, have enhanced their profile, running a station on Spitsbergen since 2002 and seeking permanent observer status at the Arctic Council. Japan has also applied for Arctic Council permanent observer status and in 2010 established an Arctic Task Force to help formulate foreign policy towards the region.

Sovereignty in international law and relations: a rejoinder

Before examining the sovereign claims of the Arctic 5, it is worth first briefly setting the scene in terms of the legal and political meaning of sovereignty in the wider world. Sovereignty is the basis of statehood and, hence, is central to the orthodox, Realist understanding of the political world as a system of states. Sovereignty became established at the 1648 Treaty of Westphalia, which ended the Wars of the Reformation that pitted Northern Protestant Europe against the Catholic South. The Protestant victory resulted in a peace treaty which asserted that Europe's kingdoms were not answerable to the Pope or any other external authority, thus enshrining the notion of sovereignty in international relations. Hence, what is often referred to as the 'Westphalian system' of sovereign states was inaugurated, a system we still have today nearly half a millennium later. In the 17th century, sovereignty was only considered relevant to Europe and so did not restrain its great powers from continuing to colonize lands outside of their continent. With the onset of decolonization in the 19th and 20th centuries, however, the Westphalian system and the notion of sovereignty as underpinning international relations became globalized. The independence of Namibia in 1990—the last colony of Africa—is often considered to mark the completion of this process. By 2013, there were 194 states in the UN covering nearly all the land mass of the world bar Antarctica. The colonies that remain—like the UK's Falkland Islands or the United States' Puerto Rico—do so because they are happy to be that way, maintaining the protection of their imperial power, whilst largely running their own internal affairs. The Arctic's one formal colony, Greenland, is grappling with this dilemma, as is explored in Chapter 4.

Politically, there are two sides to sovereignty: an internal and an external dimension.

Internal sovereignty

Internally, sovereignty refers to exclusive political control. Hence, a state's government can be referred to as the *sovereign*, in that it is the ultimate source of legal and political power. The government, be it a monarchy, dictatorship or a democratically elected cabinet, is solely responsible for making and upholding the most important laws of the land. The world's sovereign entities, of course, come in many shapes and sizes and many states devolve some powers to regional governors, but, even in the most decentralized political systems, certain key responsibilities reside exclusively with the central government and its agencies. Monetary policy and foreign policy are never devolved and sovereigns have an exclusive right to use force to uphold the law, through the enforcement agencies of the police and military forces. Hence, the use of force by non-sovereign entities (such as armed secessionist movements) is invariably denounced by the governments affected as illegitimate and 'terrorism'.

External sovereignty

The exercise of internal sovereignty also has external significance since exclusive legal and political control over a country must also mean that other governments have no right to interfere in that state's affairs. In addition to this right of non-interference, sovereignty also confers upon a country legal equality with other sovereigns including the right to be an entity in diplomacy and international law. Hence, non-sovereign entities in international relations are denied a seat and a vote in the UN and most other intergovernmental organizations and also the right to have diplomats protected by laws of immunity stationed in other states. Hence, whilst colonies of sovereign states such as Greenland and disputed territories (such as North Cyprus or Taiwan) can interact with other countries, they are not able to engage as fully in international relations as they would if they were sovereign.

What, then, distinguishes a sovereign state from any other sort of territory? In public international law, the key reference point is the 1933 Montevideo Convention, according to which a 'state' must possess:

- A permanent population
- Defined territory
- A government capable of maintaining effective control

Predictably, the third legal criteria for statehood is the most contentious and less easily defined, but the first and second are not without controversy and are enshrined in international law for a good reason. There are many uninhabited islands and tracts of land in the world that are deemed in international law to be *terra nullius*, or territory of no one. In order to avoid the potential chaos of states scrambling to claim any inhospitable chunks of rock that lie above sea level for purely economic reasons (i.e. to gain exclusive rights for extracting resources or fishing in the surrounding seas), international law considers such places to be beyond sovereign reach. The most prominent example of this is Antarctica, actually covered by a specific treaty, the 1959 Antarctic Treaty. Antarctica remains *terra nullius* in spite of the teams of scientists who periodically reside on the continent and the sometimes bizarre efforts of governments like Argentina's to assert sovereign control through acts such as flying out couples there to get married and even pregnant women to give birth. Such events are not deemed sufficient in law to constitute a permanent human occupation.

In the same year as the Montevideo Convention, a landmark ruling of the League of Nations' Permanent Court of International Justice (PCIJ) on eastern Greenland clarified the legal interpretation of sovereign occupation. The Norwegian government laid claim to east Greenland on the basis of having established settlements in 1931 in areas it claimed to be *terra nullius* and, hence, not under the sovereign jurisdiction of Denmark. When the two countries agreed to settle the dispute legally, the court found against Norway on the grounds that for over 200 years they had never contested Copenhagen's sovereignty and that the limited Danish presence in the area was reasonable given its inhospitable nature and the fact that the whole of Greenland had been included in Danish political and economic practice (PCIJ Rep Ser A/B No. 53).

Sovereignty for coastal states extends out into the sea in a series of declining levels of control as depicted in Figure 2.6. After nine years of negotiation, this practice was codified at the 1982 UNCLOS before coming into force in 1994. Prior to this, customary practice was considered to give states 3 nautical miles of territorial waters (arrived at in the 18th century as the distance that could practically be defended by coastal cannon) and, beyond that, freedom of the seas applied. After the Second World War, though, many states started to claim exclusive rights significantly further out to sea led by the United States' assertion to control the resources of its continental shelf by Truman in 1945. Inevitably, of course, many of these projections by states overlap, requiring them to resolve this by the application of the 'equidistance principle' (splitting the difference) or going to arbitration through the

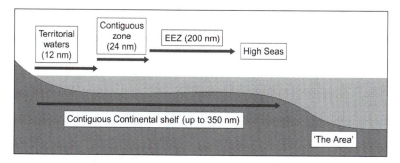

Figure 2.6 Sovereign claims and the sea
Note: nm = nautical miles

International Tribunal for the Law of the Sea, set up by UNCLOS. Exceptions to the general rule exist for Archipelagos, such as the Philippines, which can consider the seaways between their islands as internal waters, even where they exceed 12 nautical miles, and for tracts of water considered to constitute international straits essential to international navigation, such as at the Strait of Gibraltar, where the littoral state cannot restrict 'transit passage'.

UNCLOS supersedes the application of 'sector theory' in the Polar regions previously widely asserted and still advocated today by the Canadians and Russians. The basis of sector theory is that the northernmost state has sovereignty over a triangle formed from the pole and the eastern and western extremities of its territories, with allowances made for any territories falling within that zone clearly under another state's jurisdiction. Russia used this principle to annex its Arctic islands in 1916 and it still forms the basis of Canadian maritime claims outlined later in this chapter, even though the practice was declared unlawful as far back as 1933 by the PCIJ as part of its eastern Greenland ruling. UNCLOS also helped clarify the situation with regards to *terra nullius*, stating that 'rocks which could not sustain human habitation or economic life' could not be deemed sovereign territory.

Norway, Canada and Denmark are, like the Russians, claiming extended continental shelves a further 150 km from the edge of their EEZs (but not the seas or ice above). This has been done by submitting geological evidence to the UN Commission on the Limits of the Continental Shelf, a grouping of geologists elected by the parties to UNCLOS. States are obliged to submit these applications within 10 years of becoming parties to UNCLOS. Russia was the first to do so, in 2001, although it was required to re-submit the following year. Norway submitted in 2006 and the Canadians and Danes are due to submit their applications in 2013 and 2014, respectively. The United States, as a non-party to UNCLOS, is not able to make such a claim.

Much secrecy and complexity surrounds this process. In particular, there is contention about ascertaining when submarine ridges extending out from the more literal 'shelf' constitute part of that same geological mass. The lack of openness prompted Potts and Schofield to liken the process to a 'high stakes card game, though one where not only are the players unsure of the rules and thus value of their cards but where the dealer (that is, the Commission) may ultimately rule a player's hand to be essentially worthless' (Potts and Schofield 2008: 166). The Commission's findings are a technical assessment of whether a given country can legitimately claim an extended continental shelf on geological grounds. Political solutions to overlapping cases are then meant to be resolved by the countries concerned either privately or through international arbitration.

Territorial land disputes in the Arctic

There is only one territorial dispute in the Arctic region and it could lay claim to being the world's most obscure and least belligerent sovereign 'conflict'. Hans Island, a tiny islet located between Greenland and Ellesmere Island and smaller than many of the icebergs that float through the Nares Strait, has been claimed by both Denmark and Canada for the past 30 years. An amicable equidistant division of the seas between Greenland and Canada in 1973 neglected even to factor in a 1.3 sq. km rocky protrusion bisected by the line. In the succeeding years, however, the Danish and Canadian governments have both gradually built up claims to the islet with military and ministerial visits and flag-planting exercises, prompting increased media interest in both countries. Part of Copenhagen's claim centres on the fact that it was discovered in 1853 by Greenlandic explorer Hans Hendrik, after whom the islet is named. Ottawa have pointed out that Canadians have previously inhabited the rocky knoll. Both claims are correct but ultimately weak. Hendrik was actually part of a US Arctic expedition and a Canadian scientific station lasted for only a few years during the Second World War. Whilst the sovereign claims have been expressed largely in a light-hearted manner, Canadian Byers laments the 'ridiculous and expensive forms of posturing' (Byers 2010: 26) and suggests that both parties either split the islet or rule it as a condominium (ibid.: 30).

Though not a formal international dispute, Russian sovereignty over Wrangel Island, Herald Island and several nearby islets is disputed by some nationalists in Alaska and elsewhere in the United States. These islands were part of the 1867 US purchase of Alaska from Russia but had been under the control of the Soviet Union since the 1920s. The US government, though, has no claim laid for the island group and no wish to revisit the 1990 maritime agreement with the Soviet Union, which acknowledged Moscow's sovereignty over them, since the overall division of the Bering Sea made in that agreement was largely favourable to American interests.

There is the potential for climate change to usher in some new territorial claims as there are unconfirmed reports of islands north of Greenland likely to emerge with the shrinking of the ice sheet (Parker and Madid-Sadiadi 2010: 338; Potts and Schofield 2008: 160). Equally, though, it could be that climate change could render such claims obsolete as such islets are removed from the map by rising sea levels.

'Ice and a slice': territorial waters disputes in the Arctic

Bering Sea (Russia v. United States)

The delineation of the Bering Sea between the United States and Russia, referred to earlier, is still disputed despite a 1990 treaty agreeing on a division, since it has yet to be ratified by the Duma. The history of the dispute provides a neat microcosm of the shifting geopolitics of Russo-US relations over the last 160 years. The Russians, of course, brought the United States into the American Arctic equation by agreeing to sell them Alaska in 1867, the starting point of both this and the Beaufort Sea dispute. Although in the context of 20th-century geopolitics this loss of an American foothold can be viewed as an act of folly, it should be remembered that this was as much a power politics as an economic calculation by the Russians. In the 19th century, it was the British who were the Russians' key global rival, as evidenced by their preparedness to go to war with them over the geopolitical heartland of the Crimea a decade earlier. Anglo-Russian rivalry extended well beyond Eurasia to the Arctic, where the imperial possession of Canada produced a largely bi-polar balance of power. Bringing the United States into this Arctic equation was seen by the Russians as a way of weakening the British by placing their dominion in a sandwich of an emerging great power with reason to resent their imperial presence. This can easily be seen as a successful strategy given the British exit from the 'polar great game' that year when Canada was granted independence and a subsequent Anglo-American dispute over sea navigation. The United States and Great Britain agreed to go to arbitration over the Bering Sea in 1893 over the right of the United States to intercept vessels carrying out seal-culling operations restricted in US law outside of their territorial waters. The arbitration found against the United States and also against any Russian claims in the Sea beyond the three miles of their territorial waters (Sands 2003: 561–63).

The 1990 deal, hammered out between foreign ministers James Baker and Eduard Shevardnadze, was based on the terms of the 1867 purchase and epitomized Moscow's new desire to improve relations with Washington. There was great symbolic value in opening the 'ice curtain' drawn during the Cold War which had ended the long tradition of exchanges between Inuit across the short waterway. Russo-US claims in the Bering overlapped in terms of what kind of map projection was to be used. A Mercator projection favoured the Soviets, whilst a Conical projection gave the Americans a larger slice of the sea. The Baker–Shevardnadze deal split the difference between these two divisions with the exception of four 'special areas', three of which would be controlled by the United States despite being nearer the USSR, and one under Soviet control despite being nearer the United States. Since this division was generally favourable to the Americans, the Senate ratified it in 1991, but opposition in Russia has been sufficient to prevent the Duma from approving the Soviet-era deal. As referred to earlier, many Alaskans contend that the deal should have returned Wrangel Island to them, as this was part of the 1867 purchase, but the State Department have never entertained this notion and have continually reiterated their commitment to the 1990 settlement.

Beaufort Sea (United States v. Canada)

Some 21,000 sq. km of sea north of Alaska and Yukon is disputed due to the United States employing the equidistance principle but Canada sticking to the old sectoral approach, on the basis that 'special circumstances' determine that UNCLOS 1982 does not apply. In another throwback to 19th-century geopolitics, the US position is actually inherited from the Russians, the previous Alaskan landlords, and the Canadian position from their former imperial rulers the British, who reached agreement in a treaty of 1825.

Northwest Passage (United States and others v. Canada)

As already discussed, the United States, EU and others contend that the Northwest Passage should be considered international straits rather than Canadian inland waters as is the custom in international law for seas vital to international navigation. In 1970, the Pierre Trudeau government responded to the 1969 'Manhattan voyage', a transit without prior approval by US oil companies the previous year, by enacting the Arctic Waters Pollution Act, which unilaterally extended Canadian jurisdiction to 100 miles—an act never recognized by the United States. Hence, in 1985, the US *Polar Sea* again transited without prior permission from Ottawa, instead giving just 'notification'. The Northern Sea Route's status as Russian internal waters is disputed in the same way, though informally, by the United States, the EU and China.

Svalbard EEZ (Norway v. Russia and others)

The unique status of the Spitsbergen archipelago in international law, referred to in Chapter 1, under Norwegian sovereignty but open to nationals of any states signatory to the 1920 Treaty, has complicated the application of subsequent UNCLOS principles. Norwegian governments have assumed that they have a right to a 200-mile zone around the islands but other governments, most notably in Russia and Denmark, consider that the island's special status precludes such a claim. Norwegians supplement the claim by stressing that Svalbard is also on the continental shelf of their mainland. The dispute took its most serious turn in the '*Elektron* Incident' of 2005. Russian fishing vessels have regularly disregarded a 1977 Svalbard Fisheries Protection Zone, based on the EEZ, and, whilst initially this was tolerated by the Norwegians, an escalation of the practice in the 2000s prompted them to start taking legal action against the trawlers. The arrest of the captain of the *Cheringov* by the Norwegian coastguard in 2001 prompted the deployment of a Northern Fleet destroyer to the Svalbard Zone to protect Russian fishers (Åtland and Ven Bruusgaard 2009: 334–35). Four years later, Yarantov, captain of the *Elektron* trawler, resisted arrest and headed home to Murmansk with two Norwegian coastguard held captive, prompting Norwegian vessels to chase him through the Barents Sea into the Russian EEZ (ibid.: 339–40).

Lincoln Sea (Denmark v. Canada)

The 1973 Danish-Canadian delineation of the sea between Greenland and Ellesmere Island, as well as neglecting to factor in Hans Island, did not agree on a boundary north of the Nares Strait and the two country's EEZ claims have come to overlap due to differing interpretations of whether or not small islands in the strait can be used as the baselines from which to draw an equidistant line.

Overlapping extended continental shelf claims

The Russian, Norwegian, Danish and Canadian continental shelf claims overlap in several places, including the Lomonosov ridge, which runs to the North Pole, claimed by Copenhagen, Moscow and Ottawa.

The cooler reality of Arctic geopolitics

Whilst the Arctic natural environment is undoubtedly changing, the economic and political climate is not heating at anything like the rate widely predicted in 2007 and 2008.

Energy: the oil 'saunter'

Despite the way it was widely reported and commented upon, the US Geological Survey was not anything revelatory. Its findings were not out of step with previous estimates of untapped Arctic energy supplies and broadly similar to those in its 2000 report. It does appear to have been the spectacle of the robotic Russian flag-bearer that elevated the significance of the survey.

The US Geological Survey itself warns that 'no economic considerations are included in these initial estimates; results are presented without reference to costs of exploration and development which will be important in many of the assessed areas' (USGS 2008). Evaluating energy opportunities is not, of course, simply a matter of estimating the likely amounts of oil and gas under the ice and rock of the Arctic and comparing this to estimates of the rest of the world. The costs of exploration, extraction and transport are very different. The economic downturn the world has experienced since 2008 has made such costs all the more apparent and many of the companies that have acquired drilling licences for new Arctic fields have not yet set to work. For example, the Shtokman LNG field project, a much-heralded joint venture between Gazprom, TOTAL and Statoil launched in 2007 in the Russian Barents, has yet to begin operations due to the increasing doubts of shareholders prompting a series of postponements.

Even with warming temperatures, the Arctic drilling season will only be three months long for the foreseeable future. Despite its retreat, thick ice cover will be a reality in most of the Arctic for most of the year and 24-hour darkness will always be a fact of life in the winter months. Off-shore prospecting, extraction and transport is much more expensive than on-shore anywhere in the world and the costs are multiplied when in such remote locations. Shipping in the Arctic will gradually become more straightforward with warming but still not easy as the new shipping routes will only open for short seasons and an increasing number of icebergs from melting glaciers will present new hazards.

Added to all this is the fact that energy supplies are notoriously difficult to predict. There have been many false dawns in petroleum exploration. The 'deal of the century', struck by the government of Azerbaijan with eight Western MNCs in the 1990s to exploit the oil fields of the Caspian, has never lived up to expectations owing to downwardly revised estimates, political squabbling over where to locate pipelines and changes in the world price of oil. Oil finds are easily and frequently exaggerated for economic or political effect. Shares in Cairn Energy plummeted in 2010 after their preliminary report on their exploration in Greenland was released with no evidence of significant oil deposits. Arctic oil hunts have been initiated and abandoned before. The Canadian government backed private domestic companies carrying out exploratory projects off shore in the McKenzie Delta and Beaufort Sea in the 1970s but, even after several successful test drills, federal funding was withdrawn and rigs scrapped or capped off when the prohibitive costs of extraction and transport became apparent. In a broader sense, it suits Russia, the United States and Canada, and the wider community of oil importers, to give the impression to the world that they are not as reliant on Organization of the Petroleum Exporting Countries (OPEC) reserves as commonly perceived.

The political environment is also very different from the time that the US, Canadian and Russian governments could and would pour funds into speculative oil prospecting ventures. Whilst energy security concerns are rising again, the stakes are not as high as they appeared to be in the 1970s with Cold War rivalry and the rise of OPEC. In addition, the commitments of the Kyoto Protocol in limiting carbon dioxide emissions imposes additional costs on new ventures compared to the past, at least on the Canadians, Norwegians and Russians. To be added to all of these business costs is the price of fighting off the inevitable environmental protests that will accompany this most aesthetically brutal of industrial encroachments into pristine wilderness. In 2010, Cairn, irked by two Greenpeace activists who had managed to spend four days in a survival pod on a drilling platform, initiated legal actions against the non-governmental organization (NGO) for the loss of earnings they estimated at €2 million per day.

Indicative of the slow progress of Arctic oil exploration, the McKenzie gas pipeline, bringing fuel from the delta to the south of Canada and the United States, was first discussed in 1974 but has yet to be put into operation. One 'complication' here has been the need to compensate indigenous Canadians for building through lands over which they have acquired legal rights. This represents another key difference in setting up energy operations in the Arctic as opposed to most parts of Latin America or the Middle East. As is explored in Chapter 4, Alaskan Inuit have also negotiated for themselves shares in North Slope oil extraction and, even in Russia, the notionally federal structure has allowed Siberian territories to extract concessions from Moscow. The regional authority in Murmansk struck a deal with Gazprom to ensure a proportion of profits from gas extracted from the Kola Peninsula and Arhangelsk governors have a similar arrangement with Statoil linked to the construction of an on-shore base to service the Shtokman field (Mikkelsen and Langhelle 2008: 264).

The environmental and social costs of oil extraction, storage and transportation also need to be factored into the equation when speculating on the potential for a black gold rush. The 1989 *Exxon Valdez* tanker spill gave a glimpse of the particular difficulties inherent in Arctic marine pollution. Seas replete with floating pack ice and in which there is round-the-clock darkness in the winter months present particular hazards. Of greater significance than such natural factors that serve to magnify the environmental hazards posed by oil spills, however, are the social characteristics of the Arctic which make the 'response gap' bigger than for most arenas of oil industry activity. A paucity of airports, industrial ports, reliable land transport routes or emergency services make this a region ill-equipped to cope with a sudden oil rush. The scale of the 2010 Deepwater Horizon oil rig disaster (which surpassed the *Exxon Valdez* disaster as the greatest US oil spill in history), and the struggle to contain the spill served to reinforce this fear. That prospecting for new oil sources in the Mexican Gulf, with its benign climate and heavily populated and industrialized coastline, could wreak such havoc led many to speculate that a replication of such an incident off the Alaskan or Siberian coast would have far worse consequences. Environmentalists have been keen to highlight this, with the WWF commenting that 'Shell's 2010 contingency plan for a Chukchi spill identifies the village of Wainwright as the marine hub for a response effort—when Wainwright (population 494) doesn't even have a dock' (WWF 2010: 19).

The supermajor oil companies' interest in the region is not necessarily indicative of a new black gold rush. Increasingly, they have been compelled to look further afield as a result of the rise in 'resource nationalism', with the increased state control of hydrocarbon reserves. The Russian government, in particular, have acquired more direct influence over domestic energy companies and foreign investment ventures as part of the centralization that has occurred since Putin succeeded Yeltsin as president in 1999. The expertise of the supermajors is needed by the Russian government, leading to a series of cooperative international ventures at odds with the nationalistic scramble popularly portrayed and predicted.

The Russian North Pole flag-planting exercise was, like the US Geological Society survey, less dramatic politically than it appeared. It was, as Dodds notes, an act of 'stagecraft rather than statecraft' (Dodds 2010: 63). As Russian Foreign Minister Sergey Lavrov was quick to point out at the time, this was a piece of exploratory showmanship comparable to the Stars and Stripes being planted on the Moon. Indeed, it is usually overlooked that some of the money for the expedition came from Western sponsors (Baev 2010).

Making maps, not war

In April 2010, whilst President Dmitry Medvedev was visiting Oslo, the Russians and Norwegians concluded an agreement ending a low-level 40-year diplomatic dispute over how to partition the Barents Sea, amicably splitting it in two. In a joint communiqué that followed, the two foreign ministers announced: 'We firmly believe that the Arctic can be used to demonstrate just how much peace and collective interests can be served by the implementation of the international rule of law' (Store and Lavrov 2010). This initiative took much of the world by surprise but should not have done so, given that it was a win-win result. Doggedly sticking to their divergent claims had created a 'grey zone' amounting to some 12% of the Sea in which neither side could prospect for oil. A discourse analysis of policy statements and speeches in the two countries by Jensen and Skedsmo noted that behind the different tones it was 'tempting to ask whether the Norwegian and Russian approaches to the European Arctic are not that different at all' (Jenson and Skedsmo 2010: 448). In line with their relative levels of political power and democracy, Norwegian foreign policy appeared particularly discursive and cooperative, whilst Russian policy statements tend to be much more representative of a 'zero sum' approach to international political economy questions. Rhetoric and reality are not, though, the same thing when it comes to examining diplomacy. Russian policy in the Arctic has actually consistently been far less belligerent and more cooperative than portrayed in the West since the thaw evident in Gorbachev's 1987 Murmansk speech, when he declared that 'What everybody can be absolutely certain of is the Soviet Union's profound and certain interest in preventing the North of the planet, its Polar and sub-Polar regions and all Northern countries from ever again becoming an arena of war, and in forming there a genuine zone of peace and fruitful cooperation' (Gorbachev 1987). Russian overtures to the West on the Arctic have been consistently conciliatory, whilst maintaining their claims to the seas to their north. This was illustrated clearly in the ultimate resolution of probably the tensest diplomatic impasse to occur in Arctic international politics in recent years—the *Elektron* Incident. Despite some outcry amongst nationalists in the Russian media and Duma at the Norwegian arrest and pursuit of the trawler, the incident was resolved in a remarkably low-key manner. Foreign Minister Lavrov and the Northern Fleet did not react in a remotely belligerent manner and, whilst Yarantov was not given up to the Norwegians, he was later fined for illegal fishing by the Russian authorities (Åtland and Ven Bruusgaard 2009: 342–43).

The only remaining territorial question in the Arctic—over tiny uninhabited Hans Island—is a good-natured dispute and looks increasingly like being resolved by Canada and Denmark either dividing or co-ruling the icy slab. Maritime disputes still exist but this is far from unusual in international relations and there is little precedent for fighting over fish and water. Areas of contention remain in the Bering Sea between the United States and Russia, and between the United States and Canada over the Northwest Passage and Beaufort Sea, but these are lower-level disputes than the Barents Sea, which was amicably resolved. In practice, the United States and Canada have cooperated in the disputed areas with arrangements for coordinating coastguard work and special permission for navigation having been in operation since the 1980s. Again, it appears to be dawning on both sides that a compromise would be a win-win situation since the Canadian claim in the Beaufort—based on extending the territorial border northwards, whilst giving them a larger slice of the Sea up to the 200-mile EEZ limit—would also actually give them less of the sea beyond this than under the terms of the US claim—based on equidistance—because, at this distance, Canada's Banks Island comes into the equation. Hence, in a bizarre twist, the Canadian claim could favour the Americans and the US claim favour the Canadians (Byers 2011). There has been a deal on the table over the Bering Strait since 1990 but it has never entered into law due to a reluctance by the Duma to sanction what some Russian nationalists see as a sell-out to the Americans by the—in their eyes—discredited Gorbachev government. In practice, though, both sides have since stuck to the delineation agreed by foreign ministers Baker and Sheverdnadze and we again can see realpolitik for domestic consumption masking the reality of peaceful coexistence at the intergovernmental level. In addition, the stakes in the Northwest Passage dispute are not really that high. Even if it were to become an international strait it would still be 'Canadian'—it would just be that ships would not have to wait for their approval to sail through.

The continental shelf claims are being pursued in a distinctly legalistic manner with the Russians, Canadians, Danes and Norwegians patiently presenting claims to UNCLOS and showing every indication that they will abide by their arbitration. This was made public with the 'Ilulissat Declaration', which followed a meeting of the Arctic 5 in Greenland in 2008, which stated that: 'We remain committed to this legal framework [UNCLOS] and to the orderly settlement of any overlapping claims' (ILO 2008). Whilst this declaration irked the three other Arctic but not Arctic *Ocean* states—Sweden, Iceland and Finland—who were not consulted, it was very much indicative of the fact that a peaceful carve-up of the Arctic between the sovereign powers is in their mutual interests. Hence, the declaration also stated the opposition of the Arctic 5 to the alternative model of governance frequently suggested by other countries and environmentalists, of an Antarctic-style 'world park' conservation area outside of sovereign jurisdiction. Danish Foreign Minister Möller hence announced after the Ilulissat release that 'we have hopefully quelled all of the myths about a race for the North Pole once and for all' (Möller 2008).

Foreign policy statements assert national interests and zero sum characterizations of energy security because that is what foreign policy statements are supposed to do and what most of us expect to read. Formal Realism, though, often masks a truer discourse of cordial cooperative relations and that is the case with the Arctic 5. The toughest posturing has come not from the Russians or the Americans, but from Canada, but this, nonetheless, is still more rhetoric than reality. Grant suggests that 'claims of protecting Arctic sovereignty seem little more than paper sovereignty' (Grant 2010: 418), given that no new icebreakers have been constructed and a much vaunted Resolute Bay military base has not advanced in spite of the tough talk. In addition, Canadian public opinion is much more sensitive about their Arctic hinterlands than the rest of the world generally appreciates and the Harper government has actually been playing to this audience more than an international one. This was confirmed in cables released in 2010 by WikiLeaks, which, whilst revealing that geopolitics of the Middle East were perhaps even hotter than envisaged, did the opposite for the Arctic with Harper being found to admit to cordial relations with Russia (WikiLeaks 2010).

Conclusions

Rhetoric and reality are often not the same thing in international relations and particularly, it seems, in the politics of the Arctic. Arctic exploration, be it for adventure or profit, has always seemed to be accompanied by much symbolism, jingoism and bombast as man seeks to conquer nature at its most brutal in something of a 'masculinist fantasy' (Ditmer *et al.* 2011). This, though, flies in the face of the reality that making money in remote, difficult conditions necessitates cooperation rather than nationalist rivalry. Instead of the old maxim that a successful foreign policy requires one to 'speak softly but carry a big stick', what we are witnessing in the Arctic is more a case of 'talk tough but carry a big bag of carrots'. Exercising sovereign control over vast, thinly inhabited tracts of land is a difficult task. Hence, the tradition of Inuit, Sami and other indigenous groups in the region is to cooperate and share in the use of common land and resources. Arctic 'incomers' generally come to recognize the reality of this to some degree, but domestic public opinion often sees only the flags and oil-fields displayed on maps. The cordial cartel that is the Arctic 5 and the energy-seeking ventures bringing together Western MNCs and the Kremlin represent cases of transnational symbiosis rather than new Cold War nationalism. Far from the lucrative scrambles produced by the discoveries of Yukon gold of the 1920s or Alaskan oil of the 1960s, future energy exploration in the High Arctic is set to be much more long term and speculative or, as Emmerson terms it, a '(slow) rush for northern resources' (Emmerson 2010: 193). Whilst global warming is rightly bringing much-needed attention to the needs of its indigenous populations, whose lives are being altered by a transforming physical and economic climate, an awful lot of hot air has been spoken about an Arctic oil rush, territorial scramble and new Cold War.

Note

1 New York to Shanghai via Panama is 20,880 km, while via the Northwest Passage it is 17,030 km. London to Yokohama via Suez is 21,200 km, while via the Northeast Passage it is 13,841 km (Christensen 2009).

3 Globalization

Environmental change and human security in the Arctic

Box 3.1 Aleqa Hammond, Greenland government foreign and finance minister

Figure 3.1 Aleqa Hammond

'Because of the warming of the sea the halibut are multiplying faster, and the fisheries have never been so good as they are now.'

'Because of global warming our rivers and lakes have never been so full. We have lots of water and we want to use it for hydro power.'

Hammond, leader of the Centre-left Siumut Party, is a prominent political figure in Greenland and a key player in the advance of home rule. In several interviews she has raised the eyebrows of Southern observers in noting the benefits of global warming to her country's people.

(Cathcart 2007)

These comments sit uneasily with the popular view of the Arctic people and wildlife as the most tragic victims of climate change as their landscape transforms dramatically due to actions not of their own doing. Globalization is coming to the Arctic, environmentally, socially, politically and culturally at a rapid pace bringing the region literally and metaphorically in from the cold. As with the globalization that has already affected much of the rest of the world, however, this is a two-edged sword, bringing many new problems and challenges but also, at the same time, great opportunities some are keen to welcome. This chapter explores the dilemmas posed by these changes.

Introduction

Globalization is an elusive concept. It is a phenomenon so multi-faceted and chronologically opaque that its meaning is hotly disputed. At the same time, however, few deny that the international political world has been affected greatly in a variety of ways, both beneficial and harmful to certain groups of people, by what has come to be known as globalization. The notion of 'the intensification of worldwide social relations which link distant localities in such a way that local happenings are shaped by events occurring miles away and *vice versa*' (Giddens 1990: 64) could be argued to go back as far as the onset of the age of imperialism in the 15th century, or even further, but has certainly been pronounced over the last 40 or 50 years as trade, culture and policies have become more global than ever. The opportunities, problems and political paradoxes produced by this change have gradually become apparent across most of the world over the last 50 years but, in the Arctic, the impact has been more recent, whilst, at the same time, more dramatic. Industrialization, urbanization and mass tourism are coming to a region previously only sporadically touched by these phenomena and bringing with them an array of profound environmental and social changes which will transform the literal and political landscape of the High North beyond that previously seen to the south.

Environmental change in the Arctic

As discussed in Chapter 1, the Arctic has, in many ways, come to epitomize global environmental change. Pollutants almost exclusively from the south increasingly find their way into Arctic ecosystems and instigate environmental changes most keenly felt in the north. The consequences of pollution in general, most notably climate change, are most acute in the High North. Whilst such remotely engineered environmental changes are set to continue and are likely to become more acute, they are being accompanied by more direct ecological impacts from increased human activity within the Arctic.

Of course, many of the social changes brought about by industrialization, urbanization and mass tourism are broadly welcomed by many people where they have occurred in the world, and in the Arctic, too, there are great opportunities opening up as a result of these changes. Even climate change, the exemplar of global environmental catastrophe, opens up some great opportunities as well as threats. The general 'pollution or profit' paradox emerging in the Arctic has been apparent elsewhere in the world for several decades but now confronts the High North in a more pronounced fashion.

Before addressing the specifics of current environmental change in the Arctic, it is first worth recapping how such issues first emerged on the international political agenda. The globalization of environmental issues prior to their full manifestation in the Arctic can be understood in terms of the prior crystallization of some particular paradoxes in international politics.

Pollution does not respect frontiers

In the 1960s and early 1970s, ecological thought permeated into the international politics of West European and North American 'First World' states through recognition that 'pollution does not respect frontiers'. Acid rain became a contentious issue in the 1960s, not only through the emergence of evidence that rainwater could become contaminated and the effects of this on ground water and wildlife, but also because it was a problem in some states that could not be resolved by that state's government. Sulphur dioxide and other emissions from the burning of fossil fuels (coal, oil and natural gas), which accumulate in the Earth's atmosphere, can return to the surface as precipitation, hundreds of miles from where they departed as waste fumes. Hence, countries particularly suffering from this phenomenon, such as Sweden, Norway and Canada, found that they could not resolve the problem since the root cause of it lay in other sovereign states. Also in the late 1960s, the unprecedented oil spill from the *Torrey Canyon* liner off the coast of the UK served to highlight how states could be affected by pollution originating on the high seas, beyond their territorial jurisdiction and in a legal vacuum. This form of transboundary pollution most graphically demonstrated the need for international cooperation to resolve certain environmental issues, which was already obvious in the case of states sharing rivers and other forms of water.

The 'Tragedy of the Commons'

The late 1960s also saw the emergence of the idea that sovereign control over the common 'goods' of water, air and natural resources was unsustainable. In 1968, the ecologist Garret Hardin used as a parable a warning first aired in the 19th century by the economist William Foster-Lloyd on the finite quality of shared resources, known as the 'Tragedy of the Commons'. Foster-Lloyd described how the traditional English village green, conventionally open to all villagers, had become endangered because of the abuse of the privilege by the villagers in overgrazing their cattle. As the practice had gone on for centuries, it had been assumed that it always could, but it had emerged that an increase in the number of cattle above an optimum level was eroding the land and ruining the common resource for all. Hardin argued that the village green was analogous to global commons such as clean air, freshwater and high seas fish stocks, endangered by states continuing to exploit or pollute them oblivious to the fact that the cumulative effect of this would eventually be their depletion (Hardin 1968).

Local environmental problems can become global problems

From the mid-1980s, environmental policy began genuinely to globalize as changes in both the physical and political climate came to bring the First, Second and Third Worlds closer together. The ending of the Cold War brought an inclination to cooperate and also allowed space for non-strategic issues on the international political agenda, as witnessed in Mikhail Gorbachev's 1987 Murmansk initiative. In addition, however, the recognition that localized environmental problems can become global problems came to be better appreciated. Although transboundary pollution and the management of the global commons were, by the 1980s, firmly on the international political agenda, the majority of the harmful effects of environmental change were viewed as localized problems and as such were of little concern to the wider international community. Domestic legislation in the First World had banned the use of notoriously polluting chemicals like dichlorodiphenyltrichloroethane (DDT) and curbed the excesses of industrial emissions and waste disposal, leading to visible improvements in atmospheric quality and animal conservation.

However, the emergence of evidence that seemingly remote problems, experienced primarily in the Global South, had wider repercussions served to reframe some environmental issues and bring others to global political prominence. Harmful organochlorine insecticides may have been virtually eliminated from use in developed countries by the 1980s but their continued use, promoted by multinational corporations from the Global North, deprived of a domestic market, was seeing them return to their places of origin in imported foodstuffs in a 'Circle of Poison' effect (Weir and Schapiro 1981). Global, not just international solutions were required for such problems.

Environmental problems cannot be divorced from economic issues

As well as seeing some environmental issues from a wider perspective, from the 1980s, it began to become apparent that globalization in general was transforming all environmental issues. The vast majority of environmental problems are related in some way to the processes of economic development and growth, which have dominated how governments frame their policies both domestically and in the global marketplace. Industrialization and urbanization, the classic ingredients of development, put extra strains on a country's resources, whilst changing its pattern of land use and altering the balance between the human and natural environment. Increased industrial and agricultural production invariably brings more pollution as well as more raw materials, food and wealth. A United Nations (UN) commission, led by Norwegian Prime Minister Gro Brundtland, devised the notion of sustainable development as a compromise and solution to the paradox. Sustainable development reconciled environmental and economic interests by framing them as interdependent. The Global North would have to take the lead in implementing costly anti-pollution measures and recognize that the South would need more time to follow suit.

Environmental problems can have human security implications

Sustainable development and the end of the Cold War brought the world closer together intellectually and politically and served to globalize environmental politics but it was a rise of human rather than environmental interests from the mid-1980s that did most to push some of those environmental issues further up the international political agenda—'securitizing' them—through the fear that certain aspects of environmental change could be life-threatening. In 1985, the British Antarctic Survey were able to prove conclusively that the Earth's ozone layer—a protective gaseous shell in the upper atmosphere which absorbs ultraviolet rays from the Sun before they reach the Earth's surface—had a hole in it. Since such radiation can kill in the form of skin cancer and other ailments, there followed an unusually rapid international political response. Within a few months of the British Antarctic Survey discovery, the Vienna Convention on Protection of the Ozone Layer established a framework treaty, fleshed out two years later in the 1987 Montreal Protocol on Substances that Deplete the Ozone Layer. The 1987 Montreal Protocol·saw 24 industrialized states bind themselves to an agreement for major cuts in the future use and emission of chlorofluorocarbons (CFCs) and some other chemicals known to be agents of ozone depletion.

Of course, the clearest case of how environmental change can become an issue of human security is in the threat posed by global warming, which also came to be widely appreciated in the 1980s. The Earth's average temperature has risen consistently over the last century and it is now almost universally accepted that this is more than a natural development and likely to accelerate if not dealt with. The central cause of global warming is an exacerbation of the natural phenomenon of the 'greenhouse effect', caused by increased industrial emissions. Increased releases of carbon dioxide and methane over the years, principally through the burning of fossil fuels, have served to exaggerate the natural tendency of the atmosphere to trap a certain amount of infrared sunlight after it is reflected from the Earth's surface. The implications of climate change are various but include: increased desertification; a raising of sea levels due to the polar ice caps melting; the more frequent and lengthy heat waves and droughts; coastal flooding; the spread of tropical diseases north and south; ocean acidification due to carbon dioxide affecting fish stocks; more frequent and stronger riverine flooding; increased incidences of wildfires; and more frequent and stronger windstorms.

It is climate change that has most graphically brought the Arctic into focus in terms of global environmental change but all of the previously outlined paradoxes have become apparent in the High North. The Arctic is now encountering most of the same issues but at a more acute level than most of the world as several forms of environmental change have come to manifest themselves clearly:

Warming

The world's most profound form of environmental change is being felt most profoundly of all in the Arctic. In 2007, the UN Intergovernmental Panel on Climate Change (IPCC) reported that average Arctic temperatures had increased at nearly twice the global average rate over the past century and that Arctic sea ice had shrunk by 3.3% over the previous decade (IPCC 2007).

Many of the previously referenced human security impacts are coming to be felt most dramatically in the polar north due to its differentially rapid rate of warming. Pollution is being exacerbated as northerly winds become more intense, precipitation increases and the flow rate on rivers accelerates. The flow rate on the great Siberian rivers has already increased by between 15% and 20% since the mid-1980s (Usher *et al.* 2010). Further effects on pollution and the food supply are then experienced as melted ice enters the sea affecting its salinity and the ocean circulation patterns. Together with its antipodean counterpart, changes in the Arctic also contribute to the exacerbation of global warming by altering the albedo effect of the Earth, as sea ice reflects sunlight.

In addition to such polar dimensions of environmental change brought on by warming, a particular Arctic aspect of the phenomenon could come from the effects of the thaw on the atmospheric supply of methane. There are huge pockets of methane in the ground below the tundra which already account for 20% of the world's non-industrial emissions of a gas more than 20 times as powerful an agent of warming as carbon dioxide (Wille *et al.* 2008). The Western Siberian peat bog is estimated to contain around 70 billion tonnes of methane, the equivalent of 73 years of manmade carbon dioxide emissions at current rates (Pearce 2005).

Pollution

The fact that local problems can become global problems is now most graphically apparent in the High North in several forms of pollution both linked to climate change and other environmental symptoms of globalization.

Acidification

Analogous to acid rain is the 'Arctic haze' phenomenon peculiar to the High North. Arctic haze is a smog resulting from the accumulation of sulphur, nitrogen and carbon emissions in the atmosphere in winter and spring over the High North. The cold, dry Arctic air allows particles of these emissions to remain airborne for longer periods than with acid rain in temperate climes. Increasingly, this phenomenon is thought to originate more in agricultural and forest burnings in Asia than industrial emissions in Russia, Europe and North America and, hence, recent reductions in emissions prompted by international policy on climate change have not lessened the problem (Glasby and Voytekhovsky 2010: 19).

Indeed, Arctic haze is likely to accelerate with the further onset of warming and its associated social impacts in the Arctic, as it is also linked to local shipping traffic emissions as well as more distant boreal wildfires (Law and Stohl 2007).

Acidification in the Arctic has also increasingly been witnessed in the form of the eutrophication of lakes due to sulphur emissions from industrial smelting and mining. Studies have shown there to have been a progressive accumulation of sulphur in many lakes in Arctic Canada and Svalbard over recent decades. This is beyond a simple build-up of more pollutants since climate change exacerbates the phenomenon. Warming has increased the presence of algae in Arctic lakes, which is altering the traditional sulphur cycle and trapping acidifying agents in the sediment and water (Drevnick *et al.* 2010; Smol and Douglas 2007).

Oil pollution

Oil spills can occur at various levels in the process of the fuel's extraction, storage or transportation. Oil persists longer in frozen conditions so, again, this is a pollution that is more profound in the polar regions. It evaporates more slowly and can be trapped in the ice and, hence, then be released much later in melt waters. The *Exxon Valdez* environmental disaster, when a tanker hit a reef in Prince William Sound in Alaska in 1989, was one of the most notorious in history and continues to affect fishing and wildlife in the region over 20 years later. The US government tightened up regulations in the aftermath of the disaster and the threat posed by ship-source pollution does appear to have lessened. Rig spills, however, have become more frequent, with an average of 4 per year in Alaska in the 1990s growing to 22 per year by the late 2000s (WWF 2010: 4).

Ozone

Whilst the first confirmed ozone hole discovery was over the Antarctic, by 2011, evidence had emerged of a similar-sized hole over the Arctic.

This served to emphasize that, despite the phase-out of CFCs and other ozone-depleting chemicals since the mid-1980s, many of these chemicals continue to be produced and remain capable of damaging the protective layer. Unusual atmospheric conditions in the Arctic that year—ironically cooling the stratosphere—were deemed to be the root cause, illustrating that ozone depletion was not yet defeated by political action (Marshall 2011).

Persistent organic pollutants

Persistent organic pollutants, frequently referred to by the acronym 'POPs', are defined by the UN Environment Programme (UNEP) as 'chemical substances that persist in the environment, bioaccumulate through the food web and pose a risk causing adverse effects to human health and the environment' (UNEP 2009).

The chemical properties of POPs can cause them to be an environmental hazard well away from the fields where they have been used as insecticides or in industrial applications. In a phenomenon known as the 'grasshopper effect', chemicals, like DDT and carbofuran, after evaporating in the warmer climates where they tend to be used, can then be carried around the globe in the atmosphere or water in a series of 'hops' of evaporation and decomposition and then build up in food chains remote from where they are used. Since they are so slow to break down and tend to be stored in fat, POPs can end up deposited in animals thousands of kilometres from where they were used. Through the process of bioaccumulation, fish and aquatic mammals build up deposits of these toxins which can then pass through predators higher up the food chain. Hence, polar bears and wolves at the top of the Arctic food chain have been found to be contaminated by POPs, as have animals making up parts of the human diet, like seals and fish (Tenenbaum 2004).

Heavy metals

The Arctic is also prone to extreme manifestations of long-range transboundary pollution in the context of the accumulation of mercury and lead residues in food. Whilst mercury emissions from North America and Europe have progressively fallen since the 1980s due to political actions, the growth of Chinese coal-fed power plants has served to counter this and contributed to a continuation of contamination by long-range atmospheric transport which has particularly affected Arctic fish stocks, again through bioaccumulation. Mercury emissions can be transported in the air and then fall as snow in springtime and come to be ingested by seabirds and marine mammals.

Radioactive pollution

The Arctic has long been affected by pollution from elsewhere as a receptacle for the by-products of nuclear power production, both industrial and military. The 1986 Chernobyl disaster particularly affected reindeer herding in Lappland and the Kola Peninsula in the late 1980s. Radionuclides from Soviet-era testing are still detected in the Arctic today, as well as discharges from contemporary power plants, in particular the UK's Sellafield and France's Cap La Hague (Gao *et al.* 2009).

The Soviet testing of nuclear weapons and dumping of nuclear waste was particularly extensive in the northern reaches of Siberia. Some 130 tests were carried out in the Soviet Arctic between 1955 and 1970, prompting landslides and other geomorphological changes as well as depositing radioactive material in the soil, water, ice and air (Glasby and Voytekhovsky 2010: 20). Most notoriously, Novaya Zemelya was the location of the world's biggest ever nuclear explosion in 1961, when the *Tsar bomba* (Emperor bomb) was tested.

Box 3.2 The world's biggest ever nuclear explosion

Figure 3.2 The 1961 Tsar Bomba

The Arctic was the setting for the biggest ever nuclear weapon detonation when the 57-megatonne (equivalent to 57 million tonnes of TNT) hydrogen bomb, which became known as the *Tsar bomba*, was dropped by parachute from a plane on 30 October 1961 at Mityushikha Bay on the west coast of the north island of Novaya Zemlya.

As a point of comparison, this was well over 4,000 times the size of the 1945 Hiroshima explosion, which is estimated to have been around 13 kilotons. The *Tsar* was actually a 100-megatonne bomb but it was not, at the time, practical to carry out an explosion of such magnitude since delivery systems capable of firing it did not exist. It was, in addition, too big to have any real military utility since any attack on Western Europe would have produced significant fallout on Eastern Europe. The bomb, hence, was commissioned by Soviet leader Nikita Khrushchev as a political rather than military weapon symbolizing how the USSR had caught up with the United States in the nuclear arms race (Sakharov 1990).

Unlike other forms of pollution in the Arctic, however, the situation with regards to nuclear waste has improved in recent decades. Radioactive waste has decreased with the passing of time since the Chernobyl disaster and the cessation of nuclear testing (Usher *et al.* 2010).

Biodiversity

Mammals

Human-induced extinctions have, of course, provided a stark illustration of environmental damage long before the emergence of political ecology and Arctic species have been amongst those eradicated. Steller's sea cow was hunted to extinction within three decades of its discovery by Europeans in the Bering in the mid-18th century. A century later, the Great Auk, a flightless alcid bird similar in appearance to a penguin, was lost to the world as a result of the increased presence in the Arctic of hunters and bird collectors from the south who had already caused the eradication of the species in Europe.

Moving into the modern era, international concern at the replication of such a fate for the High North's best-known animal, the polar bear, culminated in a notable landmark in global environmental governance bringing together the two chief protagonists of the Cold War. The Agreement for the Conservation of Polar Bears and Their Habitats was signed in Oslo in 1973 and then ratified by the five Arctic littoral states. The agreement proscribes the hunting of polar bears by any of the parties with the exception of that carried out in the context of the traditional practices of indigenous peoples. In behavioural terms, this was a modest piece of environmental legislation. It is a soft law agreement with no enforcement mechanisms and the five states had already enacted domestic legislation restricting polar bear hunting. Indeed, the USSR had banned hunting in Arctic waters—including by indigenous peoples—as far back as 1956. However, set in context, this was a remarkable political development. The Soviets had shown little inclination to engage in the discourse of international environmental policy that had emerged from the late 1960s and boycotted the UN Convention on the Human Environment at Stockholm a year earlier. Beyond that, political cooperation of any kind between the superpowers had been thin on the ground. However, a gradual thaw in diplomatic tensions had occurred since the near disaster of the 1962 Cuban Missile Crisis had served to knock heads together and both sides were tentatively reaching out for ways to engage in dialogue and curb the spiralling costs of their arms race. Hence, the polar bear agreement was more about a mutual desire to 'improve circumpolar and international relations' (Fikkan *et al.* 1993: 96) than concern for the polar bears themselves. The symbolism of the bears as 'charismatic mega fauna' (like whales and dolphins in wider conservation agreements), added to their geopolitically benign habitat, made this unprecedented agreement possible. Like the pandas presented as gifts to mark Sino-American rapprochement at around the same time, popular big furry mammals became the icons of the new spirit of détente.

The polar bear agreement emerged from a process of scientific cooperation dating back to the mid-1960s. Concerns at increases in hunting excursions on Arctic ice flows outside of the territorial jurisdiction of the littoral states prompted the 1965 1st International Scientific Meeting on the Polar Bear at the University of Alaska. At this point, it was only in the USSR that polar bear hunting was restricted and, hence, the Soviets have to be seen as the unlikely environmental entrepreneur in this instance. The meeting called upon the polar bear states to take steps to conserve the species and exchange scientific information to facilitate this. Three years later, a Polar Bear Specialist Group was established by the International Union for the Conservation of Nature (IUCN) and it was here that the idea of the firmer commitments of the polar bear agreement arose.

Regardless of whether ultimately motivated more by anthropocentric than ecocentric values, the polar bear regime is generally held to have restricted the harvesting of these iconic mammals and aided their conservation. Today, though, the main threat to the bears comes not from the barrel of a hunter's gun but from the sun wiping out their own hunting grounds. The unprecedented rate at which ice flows are melting in the Arctic Ocean, due to climate change, is profoundly affecting the natural feeding habitats of the bears to the extent that, according to the US Geological Survey, the world's population (between 20,000 and 25,000) could decline by two-thirds by the middle of the 21st century (Armstrong *et al.* 2007). At the 2009 review of the 1973 agreement at Tromsø in Norway, it was stated that 'The parties agreed that the long-term conservation of Polar Bears depends upon the successful mitigation of climate change' (ACPB 2009).

The shift of US policy on climate change on the succession of Barack Obama as president from the denialist George W. Bush Administration found expression in a domestic policy initiative in 2010 which declared over 33,000 sq. km of the coast and sea ice of north Alaska to be a 'critical habitat' in which oil prospecting or any other non-indigenous economic activity would have to seek special federal approval. Despite the famous call by former Alaska Governor Sarah Palin to oil companies to 'drill baby drill' in the state, this marked a tempering of anthropocentric interests in the cause of ecocentric values.

Less 'charismatic' and 'mega' fauna in the Arctic have also suffered declines in their numbers. Reindeer and caribou numbers in the Arctic dropped by a third over the first 10 years of the 21st century, in spite of the 1987 US-Canada Agreement on the Conservation of the Porcupine Caribou herd. The number of wolverine is also thought to have fallen. Overall, according to the Arctic Species Trend Index, there has been a 10% decline in terrestrial vertebrates (Arctic Biodiversity 2010).

Birds

Alcids (puffins, razorbills, murres and auklets) are particularly vulnerable to poisoning by the bioaccumulation of pollutants, starving through the depletion of fish stocks and being 'collaterally killed' as by-catch in human fishing (Johnsen *et al.* 2010). In addition, there have been decreases over four decades of between 80% and 90% in the population of eider ducks, guillemots, kittiwakes and other sea birds in Greenland as a consequence of deliberate targeting after the Island's powerful hunting lobby notably persuaded the government to relax restrictions introduced in 2001 (Eccleston 2008).

Resource depletion/management

In one respect, the Arctic was well ahead of much of the world in heralding the perils of globalization in terms of the sustainable management of resources. In an early manifestation of the Tragedy of the Commons, the Viking colony on Greenland was abandoned sometime in the 14th–15th centuries due to their running out of resources. In the half millennium since this, such overt forms of colonization were not attempted and resource depletion never really manifested itself again. Climate change has altered this, however, and Greenland is now finally becoming the verdant isle the Vikings pretended it was in order to attract settlers. The Arctic today is not imminently threatened by its own Tragedy of the Commons scenario, since more of its resources are becoming available, but the fact that it is seen as a solution to global food and energy supply concerns opens up resource management issues not previously catered for.

Fisheries

The dangers posed to Arctic fish species numbers from climate change are more economic than natural since there is an expectation of an increase in fish stock changes due to northern migration. Biotic change is already occurring. Warm water plankton are known to have moved northwards by 10° between 1958 and 1999 (Jeffers 2010: 947). The principal concern is that Arctic fisheries will come to have a greater proportion of 'straddling stock' not neatly located within territorial waters, and so less subject to sovereign political controls.

There are precedents for such developments reflecting both political and environmental change. The Norwegian spring-spawning herring fishing industry dried up through the 1950s and 1960s due to overfishing, directly analogous to the overgrazing of the village green commons. More politically driven was the Bering Sea Doughnut case a few years later when US and Soviet exclusive economic zone (EEZ) declarations shrank the high seas and served to push international fishermen towards one particular fishery, which subsequently collapsed in 1972 (Jeffers 2010: 958–59).

Timber

Boreal forest (*taiga*) covers around 11% of the Earth's surface forming a broad belt below the Arctic tree line. Whilst woodlands might be expected to thrive in warmer climes, the northwards expansion of the boreal forest is doubted by many botanists due both to complex changes to the ecosystem in this region and the wider problem of deforestation through overuse (Skre *et al.* 2002).

Russia privatized the state-run forest industry in 1992, leading to an increase in both legal and illegal logging. The logging black market extends well beyond Russia and Siberian wood has regularly found its way to Japan, China and Western Europe over the last two decades.

The Chinese demand is particularly lucrative given the country's economic rise and the fact that it initiated a domestic ban on logging in 1998 due to the contribution of deforestation to flooding. As a consequence, several sawmills have sprung up near the Russian border (Humphreys 2006: 145–46).

Logging in the United States and Canada has been sustainable for some time but climate changes have already come to have some malign effects on that region's forests. An increase in wildfires has already been observed in recent decades along with the encroachment of pests such as the mountain pine beetle, prompting a rise in insect-related timber losses (FAO 2009: 42–51).

There is added, wider environmental significance with this form of deforestation because of the specific importance of boreal forests in terms of the 'carbon sink effect' and albedo. In these wooded areas, precipitation exceeds evapotranspiration, producing wetlands and lakes, meaning that a much higher proportion of carbon (84%) is stored in soils compared to tropical or temperate woodlands (IPCC 2000). Additionally, it is known that the dark pines, firs and spruces that characterize the *taiga* are significant absorbers of sunlight, thus making boreal conservation particularly important as a counter to climate change.

Encroachment

More generally, increased human encroachment in the Arctic—through industrial development and tourism—will increase environmental problems such as the accumulation of waste and less tangible forms of aesthetic and noise pollution. There are subtle biodiversity consequences of general encroachment. It has been found, for example, that reindeer retreat to at least 4 km from new roads, power lines, dams or cabins, pushing them into smaller isolated regions in which overgrazing then becomes more probable (Usher *et al.* 2010).

Globalization, health and human security in the Arctic

Human insecurities in the High North have risen through the social as well as environmental changes brought about by globalization in several ways.

Disease exposure

Increased exposure to harmful strains of disease is a well-established side-effect of globalization and it is well documented that political colonization has often been accompanied by microbial colonization.

There were sudden outbreaks of spiral meningitis, tuberculosis, influenza and pneumonia amongst Canadian Inuit in the early 1940s owing to the increased wartime presence of military and administrative staff from the south. This represented an escalation of a phenomenon previously witnessed occasionally after the arrival of supply ships from Quebec. Most strikingly, it came to be appreciated that the common cold could be fatal to natives of the polar north since these people had not developed the genetic resistance that renders this a trivial ailment in most of the world (Duffy 1988: 87–89).

Recent years have seen a resurgence of diseases in the Arctic thought to have been consigned to history in the developed world. In 2010, there were 99 recorded cases of tuberculosis in Nunavut, a rate 62 times the national average. Living standards out of step with one of the world's wealthiest countries are a contributory factor to this phenomenon but so is the biological and psychological persistence of the epidemics of the 1940s and 1950s. Many elderly Canadian Inuit carry a dormant version of the disease retained from that time, whilst memories of the clumsy and insensitive handling of the epidemics by federal authorities leave many others reluctant to undertake the lengthy antibiotic treatment courses (White 2010). Given that around 10% of Canada's Inuit were relocated in the mid-20th century (sometimes forcibly) to southern sanatoriums, from where many never returned, this is not surprising (Grygier 1994).

Food security

In a side-effect to the rise of pollution in the region, sometimes referred to as the 'Arctic dilemma', health problems have arisen as a result of people consuming less of their traditional foodstuffs through fears of poisoning by lead, mercury or POPs. The relative poverty of native Arctic peoples allied to the relatively high costs of non-local foods due to their long-range transport makes the 'nutrition transition' away from their traditional diet particularly damaging. The types of 'Western' foods best suited to long-range transport are, of course, not fresh fruit and vegetables but processed snacks like crisps, biscuits and fizzy drinks, which bring with them several negative health consequences.

Lifestyle illnesses

The globalization of culture also explains the appeal of Western food and this has served to heighten health insecurity in the Arctic. A rise in rates of obesity and diabetes has resulted from the nutrition transition to Western consumption patterns. The mechanization of travel and decline in hunting in some communities has also added to the obesity problem as the Arctic lifestyle has become less active (Sharma 2010).

Native Alaskans are nearly nine times more likely to die of alcohol-related health problems than the average US citizen (Seale *et al.* 2006). Cancers were near non-existent in the Arctic until the last 100 years, but lung, colon and breast cancers have soared due to social change (Friborg and Melbye 2008). Lung cancer rates in the Canadian Inuit are the highest in the world, with over half of them having taken up smoking (Krummel 2009: 515).

Suicides

A classic indicator of social malaise is the rate of people taking their own lives and this is striking across the Arctic. Suicides amongst northern natives in Russia are over three times that for the overall population of a country with one of the world's highest rates. East Greenland has one of the highest regional rates in the world at 1,500 per 100,000 (Krummel 2009: 511). A Canadian report found that sui-cide rates amongst male Nunavut Inuit between the ages of 19 and 24 were around 50 times that found in the equivalent demographic group in the rest of the country. Although stereotypically explained by cold, dark and lonely lifestyles, suicide is very much a product of globaliza-tion and was comparatively rare in the Arctic in the pre-modern age. There was only one suicide in Nunavut in the whole of the 1960s but, since then, the 'historical trauma' of rapid social change has seen young men exposed to the forms of alienation linked to depression in the developed world—educational failure, sexual frustrations, the use of alcohol and drugs, and petty crime—but to a much greater degree. Mental illnesses are not 50 times more prominent in young Nunavut men, so explanations have to be social rather than biological and pat-terns of social change appear to support this. Suicide began to rise significantly in the Alaskan Inuit in the 1960s, the Greenland Inuit in the late 1970s and then the Nunavut Inuit in the 1980s, at the same time as modernization, in the form of colonial education, settled com-munities and a decline in traditional hunting employment, set in (Nunavut 2008: 16–17).

Globalization has brought new opportunities for Arctic peoples but has also rendered them more vulnerable to a range of new insecurities. The uneven nature of globalization witnessed worldwide is also illustrated in microcosm since Inuit life expectancy is considerably lower than the average for citizens in the Arctic states. In Canada and Greenland, the difference is more than 10 years. Life expectancy for Canadian men, for example, is 77.2 but for Inuit in Nunavut it is just 66.6 (Krummel 2009: 509).

The regional governance of environmental change and human security

As international environmental policy has evolved since the early 1970s, two very different solutions to the resultant paradoxes have emerged. First, you can have a Liberal solution: informed collective management to regulate use of the commons for the benefit of all. Second, in a more Realist solution, you can abandon the idea of the commons and, instead, divide land and resources up into individual holdings in the expectation that each 'plot holder' would graze and use resources sustainably. Both types of solutions are evident in the development in the 1970s and 1980s of international law for a 'commons' already subject to many centuries of contention, the high seas (seas outside of any state's jurisdiction). The Third UN Conference on the Law of the Sea (UNCLOS III), which concluded in 1982, included an agreement that minerals on the bed of the High Sea would be the property of a new International Seabed Authority. This form of collective management to sustain collective goods can, however, be contrasted with the encroachment on the tradition of the 'freedom of the seas' by the huge growth of waters claimed by states in the legitimization at UNCLOS III of 200-mile EEZs. An EEZ does not denote the full sovereign control of *territorial waters* (12 miles from the coast), but gives the state concerned primary rights over fishing and mineral exploitation in the zone. The rationale offered for the creation of EEZs was that fish stocks and other resources would be utilized more sustainably if under sovereign jurisdiction rather than subject to a 'free for all'. A tension between the 'freedom of the seas' and sovereign management persists and looks set to become more acute in forthcoming years as a number of states look to extend the EEZ principle to continental shelves beyond 200 miles of their coastlines. Arctic policy has similarly evolved in both Realist and Liberal directions. EEZ logic has been extended through the continental shelf and re-asserted sovereign claims discussed in the previous chapter. The focus on this, though, has tended to obscure plentiful evidence of Liberal cooperation dating back even to the Cold War era.

Issues of environmental change and human security are notable for exposing the limits of state governance and the necessity of international cooperation. This rationale was the spur for Arctic political cooperation but so were the more conventional, intergovernmental motives that this realm of diplomacy offered in terms of fostering peaceful relations between the Cold War superpowers. This was apparent with the Polar Bear Convention at the end of the first phase of the Cold War in the early 1970s, and was then revived with the westward overtures of Gorbachev at the end of the second Cold War in the late 1980s. Gorbachev's 1987 Murmansk speech included international environmental cooperation as one of its six key proposals. The 1989 Rovaniemi preparatory meeting of the 'Arctic 8', which arose out of Gorbachev's initiative, then laid the foundations for the Arctic Environment Protection Strategy (AEPS) launched two years later.

> The Soviet Union proposes drawing up jointly an integrated comprehensive plan for protecting the natural environment of the North. The North European countries could set an example to others by reaching an agreement on establishing a system to monitor the state of the natural environment and radiation safety in the region. We must hurry to protect the nature of the tundra, forest tundra and the northern forest areas.
>
> (Gorbachev 1987)

The AEPS identified six priority problem areas: POPs, oil pollution, heavy metals, noise, radioactivity and acidification. Four working groups were also established by AEPS: the Arctic Monitoring and Assessment Programme (AMAP); Conservation of Arctic Flora and Fauna; Protection of Arctic Marine Environment (PAME); and Emergency Prevention, Preparedness and Responses (EPPR). The AEPS was later absorbed into the Arctic Council, adding a fifth working group, Sustainable Development. These five groups today represent the key forums for international political cooperation and epistemic consensus-building on Arctic environmental issues. This system is analysed in Chapter 5.

Outside of the Arctic Council system several environmental regimes aid environmental governance in the Arctic, which are summarized in Box 3.3. A notable absence among these agreements is a regional application of the global marine pollution regime MARPOL. An amendment of the 1990 International Convention for the Prevention of Pollution from Ships that sets limits on permissible discharges recognized Antarctica and many seas as 'special' areas, in terms of their vulnerability to pollution, but this designation has never been given to the Arctic. The Arctic is hence covered by the standard restrictions but not yet the more stringent versions.

Box 3.3 International environmental agreements relevant to the Arctic

Pollution

UNCLOS: The Arctic is recognized as a special area under Article 234 of the Law of the Sea. Arctic states have extended environmental protection rights in a given region (i.e. can restrict international shipping) if ice is present in the sea for most of the year. The UN's International Maritime Organization, which administers UNCLOS, has also developed the 'Polar Code', an unofficial understanding between the Arctic states on specific safety precautions for shipping in Arctic waters.

LRTAP: The Convention on Long Range Transboundary Air Pollution came into force in 1983 and has been expanded by several protocols to commit over 50 states (including the Arctic 8) to curbing emissions of pollutants such as those that cause acid rain and Arctic haze.

Stockholm Convention: The International Legally Binding Instrument for Implementing International Action on Certain Persistent Organic Pollutants (POPs Treaty) was signed by 127 governments at a diplomatic conference in Stockholm in May 2001 and entered into force in 2004. Under Article 8 of the Convention, a Persistent Organic Pollutants Review Committee appraises proposals to add new chemicals to the original 12. The Convention is an example of 'soft international law' in that it is legally binding but contains no enforcement measures. Russia and the United States, though, are not parties.

OSPAR Convention: The Convention on the Protection of the Marine Environment of the North East Atlantic came into force in 1998 committing 16 parties to prevent pollution from activities other than fishing and shipping.

Barents Euro-Arctic Region Regime: This evolved from bilateral Russo-Norwegian cooperation in the thawing political atmosphere of the 1980s and, from its inauguration in 1994, the Barents Euro-Arctic Council (examined in more detail in Chapter 5), consisting of Denmark, Finland, Iceland, Norway, Russia, Sweden and the European Union (EU), has facilitated cooperation and funding for projects on pollution and biodiversity through an Action Plan and Working Group on the Environment.

Biodiversity

Ramsar Convention on Wetlands: This identifies several designated protected wetland areas in the Arctic, including Queen Maud Gulf Nunavut and others in Svalbard, Greenland and Siberia.

CITES: The Convention on the Trade in Endangered Species restricts the trading of plant and animal specimens that are in danger of extinction. Narwhal and beluga whales are amongst fauna covered in the 'Red Lists' of endangered species.

Convention on Migratory Species: A UNEP-managed, species-specific regional agreement on migratory birds. However, only the Nordic four of the Arctic 8 are parties.

IUCN Red Lists: These highlight endangered species of flora and fauna listed by the International Union for the Conservation of Nature as requiring conservation measures. Those native to the Arctic include the beluga whale, Arctic wolf, polar bear, Arctic hare and Arctic ground squirrel.

UNESCO Convention Concerning the Protection of the World's Cultural and Natural Heritage: This Convention includes amongst its designated sites one cultural and four natural locations in the Arctic.

Joint Norwegian-Russian Fisheries Commission: This evolved from informal cooperation that crossed Cold War lines with joint quotas set by Oslo and Moscow from 1976 to sustainably co-manage cod, haddock and capelin stocks in the Barents.

North Atlantic Marine Mammals Commission: An agreement between Norway, Iceland, Greenland and the Faeroe Islands to co-manage whales, seals and walruses.

The Arctic notably lacks the systematic and comprehensive environmental governance of its antipodean counterpart, the Antarctic Treaty. Greenpeace in 2012 launched a 'Save the Arctic' campaign calling for this, and some intergovernmental voices have also advocated such a development. An EU-funded research project, for example, concluded that:

> the existing patchwork of conventions and agreements will not adequately facilitate sustainable management of the Arctic marine

area in the near future. To address this challenge, multiple new initiatives aim to integrate and coordinate governance, spanning from the country, to circumpolar to global levels and including governmental and non-governmental stakeholders such as the indigenous peoples, industry and environmental organisations.

(Roo *et al.* 2008: 3)

The all-encompassing Antarctic model of environmental governance is, however, something of a frozen red herring. Other than being cold and polar, the fact is that the Arctic and Antarctic have very little in common and there is little to be learned from the environmental success story that is the 1959 Treaty. Outlawing sovereign claims and economic development in a continent with no indigenous population and limited economic attraction to the states of the world cannot be compared to doing so in a region that is more than just a planetary opposite. Greenland, Svalbard, Nunavut and the coasts of Alaska, Siberia, Northwest Territories and Yukon are not *terra nullius*—they are under the sovereign jurisdiction of economically developed and powerful states and long inhabited by thousands of people. There is about as much chance of the Russians and Americans giving up Alaska and Siberia to become part of a world park as there is of them handing over Hawaii to the Japanese or Kaliningrad to the Germans or Poles. Whilst the messy hotch potch of legal instruments that currently characterizes Arctic governance lacks the neatness of a single binding international treaty, it may be that such arrangements carry more likelihood of enhancing environmental governance and human security in the changing Arctic. Oran Young, that most renowned scholar of both environmental governance and Arctic politics, is certainly of that opinion:

What makes sense is to aim for the development of a regime or governance complex in the sense of a set of linked arrangements that are capable of addressing specific issues on their own but that also add up to a comprehensive governance system for the region. Thus we can work towards the development of a Polar Code under the auspices of the International Maritime Organization to govern Arctic shipping; a more informal collection of best practices relating to the extraction of oil and gas in areas under the jurisdiction of individual Arctic states; one or more regional fisheries management organizations dealing with specific areas of interest to fishers; and a code of conduct applying to Arctic tour operators.

(Young 2011b: 192)

Any 'hard law' Arctic Treaty that could be concluded could only come about with the consent of the Arctic powers and so, inevitably, would reflect traditional sovereign interests as seen from capitals far to the south of the polar circle. Soft law arrangements and international regimes instinctively seem like second-best legal solutions to problems but increasing evidence in environmental and human rights regimes suggests that these are more likely to be informed by human and environmental interests than formal intergovernmental agreements. As discussed in the previous chapter and illustrated in later chapters, governments the world over tend to be more cooperative and flexible when they are away from the spotlight of high-profile international diplomacy.

4 Decolonization

'The cold wind of change'

Box 4.1 The 'Sami *Magna Carta*'

Figure 4.1 King Frederick V of Denmark-Norway

Until the middle of the 18th century, 'Lappland' was untouched by the notion of sovereignty which had spread over most of the rest of Europe since its establishment at the Treaty of Westphalia a century earlier. In 1751, however, the Nordic states resolved to establish territorial borders through their northern hinterlands as an appendix to the Strömstad Treaty which agreed the overall delineation of the frontiers of Sweden, Finland and Denmark-Norway (then a single kingdom). In the *Lappekodicill* (Lapp Codicil), Denmark-Norway and Sweden agreed that some exceptions to their Scandinavian carve-up would apply to the Sami. King Frederick V of Denmark-Norway (pictured) had previously commissioned research into the interests of the nomadic Sami in the 1740s and, based on this, in an exercise of democracy and self-determination out of step with the rest of Europe at the time, a right to roam was established.

> The Sami need the land of both states. Therefore, they shall, in accordance with tradition, be permitted both in autumn and spring to move their reindeer herds across the border into the other state.
>
> Whilst the Strömstad Treaty meant the Sami of Lapland (Sapmi) must now become Danish-Norwegian or Swedish citizens, the *Lappekodicill* was, nonetheless, a remarkably foresighted statement of the rights of indigenous peoples and set an important legal precedent for the recognition of the Sami as a nation distinct from the Swedes, Norwegians and Finns that is still relevant today.

Introduction

Self-determination movements are prominent in all five major Arctic states and, to a lesser extent, in Sweden and Finland also. These movements have long histories but, compared to other colonies and peripheral regionalist groupings elsewhere in the world, have proven to be more modest in aim and strategy. As outlined in the previous chapter, globalization has served to bring new threats to the livelihoods and culture of Arctic indigenous peoples and, as a result, kindled nationalist sentiments previously only very sporadically witnessed. Paradoxically, globalization has also served the cause of the High North's original inhabitants by making the world more aware of them and giving them a platform to assert their identities and rights in a sophisticated manner in keeping with a changing world. This new 'Cold Wind' of formal and informal decolonization is thus more restrained than most of the nationalist movements that have shaped the political world over the last 200 years but may, nonetheless, prove to be among the most successful, in spite of occurring in the context of asymmetries of power beyond any previous self-determination struggles. Tiny unarmed movements have been able to extract significant autonomist concessions from some of the world's most powerful states in a phenomenon that looks likely to continue in spite of (and, indeed, because of) the recent rise of metropolitan interest in their northern fringes.

The Sami

The Sami (Lapps) are one of the oldest ethnic groupings in Europe and generally are held to be the original inhabitants of northern Scandinavia (or culturally *Sapmi*, or geographically *Fennoscandia*), present in the region before the arrival of the Vikings and Finns. Sami today number between 70,000 and 100,000 (assimilation makes a precise figure impossible), with 40,000–60,000 living in Norway (mainly in Finnmark), 5,000–20,000 in Sweden, 9,000 in Finland and 2,000 on the Kola Peninsula in Russia.

As with the onset of imperialism in other parts of the world, the story of colonial domination in 'Lappland' followed three broad phases, moving from informal and sporadic attempts to modernize and control the region through formal colonization to a present post-colonial phase. Territorial claims in the region began to be asserted by the kingdoms of Norway, Sweden and Finland from the 13th century and Christian missionaries also began seeking to convert the largely shamanist Lapps. The nomadic Sami would sometimes find themselves taxed simultaneously by three crowns, but most managed to avoid paying any and remained largely free from foreign domination until sovereign 'order' began to be imposed from the 19th century (Sandberg 2008: 274).

Norway as a whole was colonized between the 16th and 19th centuries when its kingdom was absorbed by the Danish crown. However, the

Figure 4.2 Map of *Sapmi*

Norwegians gained a measure of home rule in a monarchical union with Sweden from 1814 and the embryonic modern Norwegian 'state', imbued with liberal nationalism, tended to treat the Sami as fellow anti-colonialists. The new Norwegian government and constitution demonstrated an early commitment to multi-culturalism, spawning policies acknowledging Sami linguistic and educational rights. Upper-class Norwegian landowners in Finnmark, however, viewed their part-nomadic co-habitants quite differently and became the key proponents of a government policy of 'Norwegianization' to modernize and standardize the behaviour of the Sami in order to secure exclusive economic rights over their holdings (Minde 2005: 11). This policy lasted for over 100 years from the middle of the 19th century, growing more virulent over time. The *Finnefondet* ('Finn Fund', since the Sami are ethnically related to the Finns) was initiated in 1851 to promote the use of the Norwegian language amongst the Sami, although it was not, at this stage, accompanied by the systematic suppression of Sami language and culture.

Although formal Norwegianization was in its infancy, tension arising from a culture clash between the Sami and settlers from the south had already been building and manifested itself in the only violent episode in the history of Sami nationalism in the Kautokeino uprising, a year after the introduction of the policy in 1852. In a dramatic and uncharacteristically aggressive episode, the subject of a feature film in 2007, a posse of Sami men, women and children marched on and attacked the town's sheriff, liquor merchant and priest, killing the former two. The precise motives for the uprising are disputed but, as with many historical and contemporary cases of politically motivated non-state violence, a combination of cultural resistance to foreign domination and religious fervour appears to have been unleashed. The mob, adherents to a new puritanical sect of Laestadianism, a fundamentalist offshoot of the Lutheranism of the Norwegian State Church, were particularly offended by the sale of liquor to Sami, amongst whom alcoholism had become a major problem. The Norwegian State Church was seen as complicit in this trade. Fellow local Sami eventually stopped the mob who were then arrested, with two of their number, including leader Aslak Haetta, later beheaded.

Norwegianization hardened from the 1880s with teachers instructed to restrict the use of the Sami (and Kven Finnish) language in schools and many Sami children sent to boarding schools away from their homeland. In 1902, an act made land ownership open only to citizens literate in Norwegian which was blatantly discriminatory since many Sami did not fit the stereotype of nomadic herders and were interested in becoming farmers. In a manner comparable to many new states, full independence in 1905 saw Norway move further from romantic liberal nationalism to integral, assimilationist nationalism, with Sami and Kven differences increasingly viewed as a problem to the Norwegian 'national interest'. In particular, these people came increasingly to be constructed as a potential security threat because of their ethnic link to neighbouring Finland or because they represented a weak spot in the new state that could be exploited by the Russians (Minde 2005).

Mirroring the way that elsewhere in Europe nationalism had largely transformed from a modern liberal emancipatory ideology to the ultra-conservative, chauvinistic forms that characterized the first half of the 20th century, Sami assimilation in Scandinavia also came to be influenced by Social Darwinism. In Sweden, where a similar strategy towards the Sami as Norway's had been adopted from the mid-19th century, policy actually moved from paternalist assimilation to segregation with separate 'nomad schools' for Sami established in 1913 providing a rudimentary education in tents. The survival of the fittest mentality was at this time popular in liberal as well as fascist circles and, hence, a country that came to be a world leader in welfare and democracy established the world's first state-sponsored Institute for Race Biology at Uppsala in 1921 and embraced eugenics in a policy of sterilizing the mentally ill and socially 'deviant' from 1934.

Attitudes to indigenous minorities gradually changed after the Second World War as both the Nordic social democracies and the Sami themselves embraced emergent international notions of economic and social rights and multi-culturalism. The north of Norway was particularly devastated in the war as a result of a German scorched earth policy and this, along with their notable contribution to Norwegian resistance, helped to change attitudes towards the Sami, as it had done towards colonial subjects and the working classes in much of the Western world.

The Sami Reindeer Association was formed in 1947 and formal pan-Nordic Sami cooperation was inaugurated at a conference in Jokkmokk, Sweden, in 1953, paving the way for the Nordic Sami Council, founded three years later in 1956. In the same year, a Sami Committee of the Norwegian government was established, dealing with cultural and linguistic concerns, marking an end to Norwegianization. With their voice now able to be heard, a Sami rights movement came to mobilize around the issue of several state damming projects being developed in Finnmark. The construction of the Alta-Kautokeino dam and hydro-electric power station in the late 1970s and early 1980s was the particular catalyst for a series of reforms empowering the Sami. Protests by Sami groups and environmentalists initiated in the early 1970s intensified between 1979 and 1982 with hunger strikes even occurring outside the Storting (parliament) in Oslo. The government pushed through with the construction but the movement was not in vain as the scale of protest shocked Norwegians and prompted a state inquiry on the question of Sami rights. A commission led by Law Professor Carsten Smith recommended the ideas of a Sami parliament and an amendment to the 1814 Norwegian Constitution, and culminated in the landmark reformist Sami Act of 1987.

Hence, Sami rights were added to the Constitution in 1988 and a Norwegian Sami parliament (Samediggi) was established in 1989, replacing an appointed and limited Sami Council that had been created in 1964. In 1990, a language act officially recognized the Sami tongue and a further reform saw a secretary of state for the Sami created as a permanent position in the Oslo government in 1997. The Samediggi in Karasjok comprises thirty-nine members elected every four years from seven constituencies covering all of Norway. Responsibilities have grown over time to include the management of the Sami Development Fund; linguistic, cultural and educational rights; and co-management of the 'Finnmark Estate' (95% of land in the county) alongside the Council.

In a clear instance of political spill-over, Sami parliaments were then established in Sweden and Finland in 1993 and 1995, respectively (though the act of parliament establishing the Finnish body was as far back as 1973). The Swedish body in Kiruna has 31 members elected every four years, whilst the Finnish parliament has 20 representatives from the Sami domicile area elected for four-year terms, based in Inari. The Finnish and Swedish Sami parliaments are more limited than their Norwegian counterpart and the legal status of the people is similarly less advanced. A report by the United Nations' (UN) Human Rights Council has commented that Sweden has made 'limited progress in resolving Sami rights issues' in relation to overcoming tensions between land ownership and grazing rights and protection of the language (Anaya 2011: 34). Around 90% of designated Sami 'homeland' in Finland is still owned by the state and neither Finland nor Sweden has ratified International Labour Organization (ILO) Indigenous and Tribal Peoples Convention 169, whilst Norway was the first government to do so.

In mitigation, the Swedes and Finns can point out that their Sami populations are smaller and less geographically or socially distinct than in Norway. Equally, despite lagging behind their Western neighbour, there is little doubt that the rights of Swedish Sami have been enhanced in recent times. In 2011, a Constitutional amendment came into effect recognizing the Sami as a 'people' and the Swedish Supreme Court came to a landmark verdict upholding the rights of Sami in Västerbotten to allow their reindeer to graze against a powerful lobby of local landowners attempting to sue them for damage.

In fact, the Human Rights Council report, whilst recognizing that indigenous rights in Scandinavia were amongst the most advanced in the world, expressed some doubts as to the 'parliamentary' credibility of even the Norwegian body, commenting that all three are 'generally regarded as bodies through which the Sami can express their voice to government authorities, without any guaranteed genuine influence or decision making power' (Anaya 2011: 11). There is, though, no doubt that force of example has been a factor in Sami rights spilling over from Norway to its Nordic neighbours and this has now extended even, to a limited extent, to Russia. In 2010, a nine-person Kola Sami Assembly was established within the Murmansk Oblast at its second Sami Congress, following its initiation in 2008. Doubtless, there is some way yet to go in this story of Sami rights and autonomy but, through reference to the existence of disparities in national laws and the emergence of international laws, they are set to be empowered further.

Denmark: Greenland

Box 4.2 Timeline of Greenlandic home rule

982	'Discovery' by Erik the Red—a Viking Icelander (other humans had previously settled—most recently the Dorset Inuit—but the island was uninhabited at this point)
986	Viking settlement established by Erik
1200±	Arrival of Thule Inuit from Canada
1261	Becomes a Norwegian crown possession
1380	Becomes a Danish/Norwegian crown possession
1500	End of the Norse settlement
1721	Formally colonized by Denmark after the arrival of missionary Hans Egede
1953	Annexation—becomes a province of Denmark
1979	Home rule
2009	'Self-government'

Contrary to what might be assumed, it was the Inuit who were the colonizers and the Vikings the vanquished aborigines in Greenland. Historical sources are thin but it appears that the Vikings failed to adapt to falling temperatures that came with the onset of the Little Ice

Age of the late 15th century and, refusing to trade with or learn from their un-Christian *'skraeling'* (wretch) neighbours, left them to control the island (McGovern 1980; Diamond 2005: 248–76).

Although technically Greenland had been a Danish colony for over three centuries, as a consequence of their royal union with Norway, a formal colonization did not occur until the 1720s in the wake of visits by Christian missionaries. Economic interests were soon asserted on the giant island with the Danish crown assuming responsibility for Greenlandic trade in 1726 and then, 50 years later, the Royal Greenland Trading Company established to further economic control from Copenhagen (Petersen 1995: 119).

A tightening of Danish control over the island then took place after the Second World War, during which sovereignty had effectively been ceded to the United States for defence purposes, which proved to be the catalyst for Greenlandic nationalism. The achievement of independence from Denmark for neighbouring Iceland in 1944 provided an added source of inspiration. In contrast to their stance over Iceland, however, the Danes annexed Greenland in 1953 after holding a referendum in the 'mother country' but not the colony (Petersen 1995: 120). That year also saw the establishment of a US airbase at Thule with Inuit forcibly removed from the area to make way for the 'security guarantors'. This US military occupation became contentious again in 1968 when a B52 plane crash released radiation and also evidence that a US nuclear arsenal was secretly stationed on Greenland.

Accompanying such evidence of policies being decided over their heads was a social change undermining the Inuit character of Greenland. Under the policy of 'Danization', the Danish population grew from around 4% in the early 1950s to 20% in the 1960s due to incentives given to settle (Petersen 1995: 121). This more visible and social colonization created the first real incarnation of Greenlandic nationalism. The provincial council of Greenland lobbied the government in Copenhagen for greater powers, prompting them to set up a commission of Danish and Greenlandic politicians to consider the proposition. This commission recommended home rule, which was then put to the island in a referendum and 70% of Greenlanders voted for this in 1979. Some 21 years on, 76% then voted for more extensive 'self-government', establishing a new parliament, the Landsting, and government, Landsstyne, with far-reaching powers including authority over taxation, fishing and education. Hence, since 2009, self-determination has been enshrined with the acknowledgement by Copenhagen that, although they retain formal sovereignty, full sovereign independence will be a decision to be taken by the Greenlandic people alone.

Whilst full sovereign independence may appear the next logical move for Greenland, several factors do mitigate against taking this final step.

The Danish subsidy

Greenland is subsidized by Copenhagen to the tune of 3,495 million Danish krona per year (nearly €470 million). This amounts to one-third of the country's gross domestic product (GDP) or over €8,000 per person, and is money that would disappear on the advent of full sovereignty (Statistics Greenland 2011).

European Union (EU) links

Although they famously became the first and only country to withdraw from the European Community in 1985, following a referendum arranged after gaining home rule, Greenland has maintained important links with the evolving Union. Under the 'Greenland Treaty', under which its withdrawal was managed, the island became one of the Community's 'overseas countries and territories' and so entitled to development aid.

> ... arrangements being introduced which permit close and lasting links between the Community and Greenland to be maintained and mutual interests, notably the development needs of Greenland, to be taken into account.
>
> (EEC 1985: preamble)

This aid has amounted to a sum of €42.8 million per year from 2001. Between 2001 and 2006, this was in the context of a fisheries agreement, but, since 2007, when the five-year EU Partnership Programme was established, this sum now includes €25 million per year developmental support for Greenland's education system and access to EU education and research programmes. Hence, some would say receiving EU subsidies without being constrained by its restrictive fisheries policy was the best of both worlds for Greenlanders and not something they should forgo lightly.

North Atlantic Treaty Organization (NATO) defence

Danish sovereignty also brings to Greenland the security guarantee of the world's premier military power and military alliance. Denmark is probably the most Atlanticist state in Europe and its consistently close alignment to the United States has ensured that any Soviet or Russian strategic interest in the island has never been an option. Greenland, indeed, epitomizes the famed view of NATO's first Secretary-General Lord Ismay on the role of the alliance to 'keep the Russians out, the Germans down and the Americans in', since the US role was initiated to thwart Germany during the Second World War. The 1941 Agreement Relating to the Defense of Greenland recognized Danish sovereignty but gave the United States a free hand in terms of military activities on the island. Denmark's US Ambassador Henrik Kauffmann signed the treaty but was rebuked by the government in Copenhagen for exceeding his authority (Taagholt and Hansen 2001: 23). Following the inauguration of NATO two years previously, the 1941 Treaty was replaced by the 1951 Defence Treaty which essentially continued to give the Americans a free hand, albeit this time with some limited Danish involvement in the security bases. The US military presence on the island has not been without controversies but there is little doubt that this side-effect of Danish sovereignty has provided Greenland with as strong a defence as any country of the world. An independent Greenland would take them outside of NATO, out from under the United States' missile shield and give the Americans less reason to protect them if ever they were to need it. The fact that the United States also pays rent for the privilege of defending Greenland gives an extra financial incentive to retaining home rule without full sovereignty. If the Danish special relationship is taken out of the equation, the commitment of Washington could wane, as witnessed in neighbouring Iceland when its base in Keflavik was closed and permanent troops withdrawn in 2006. At a stroke, Iceland lost hundreds of jobs, millions of dollars and, arguably, its defence, as it possesses no national armed forces.

Danish 'know how'

Denmark may be a relatively small country but it is not an insignificant player in the political world due to its high standard of living and EU and NATO membership. Danish experience in international trade, diplomacy and administration might be too easily abandoned in the face of huge economic and political changes arising from a sudden influx of multinational corporations (MNCs) and foreign government interest. Aqqaluk Lynge, president of Greenland's Inuit Circumpolar Council (formerly Conference) (ICC), voicing concerns over a lack of the democratic infrastructure necessary to control MNCs and ensure environmentally responsible development, has warned: 'We have to be careful we don't pay a terrible price for our independence' (Windeyer 2010).

Since they subsidize Greenlanders to the tune of US$11,000 per person, Danish political and public opinion is torn between seeing the island as a giant millstone or a future stepping stone to Arctic riches, but the die is now cast and the decision rests with the islanders.

Self-government has not been plain sailing and internal divisions on future governance have emerged. One-time ICC colleagues Lynge and current Prime Minister Kuupik Kleist increasingly have found themselves in separate corners, with the former asserting that the premier has 'sold out', literally and metaphorically, by ushering in MNCs and abandoning the Inuit tradition of common land ownership. There is no tradition of private ownership of land in Greenland but the Kleist government has come to challenge common ownership of land as the Danes had previously tried. Controversies have emerged from this such as the arrest of several Inuit in recent years who had been hand-collecting rubies on sites sold by the government to MNCs. Many of the younger generation and 'urbanites' of Nuuk buy into Kleist's vision of bringing in MNCs to modernize the country and dream of becoming a 'new Saudi Arabia'. Lynge, on the other hand, has cautioned about the dangers of the 'resource curse' making Greenland some sort of dysfunctional 'Nigeria of the Arctic': 'When I'm lying awake at night, I pray we don't find oil' (Kucera 2009). This view is echoed by many older and rural-dwelling Greenlanders who are, in general, more cautious and fear the consequences of rapid social and economic change.

Who, then, are the nationalists? The Inuit traditionalists wanting to maintain their people's identity against the encroachment of the south, or the Inuit modernists seeking to cut the umbilical cord from Copenhagen by radically changing their country and embracing the ways of the south? This is the dilemma of pursuing sovereignty in a world when the very concept is in flux.

United States: Alaska

Alaska was only absorbed into the United States as the 49th state as recently as 1959, having been a colony since 1867 when the US government purchased the territory from Russia, with a treaty that makes just one reference to the native population, who are described as 'uncivilized tribes'. The 1958 Alaska Statehood Act, however, showed that much democratic progress had been made in North America over the previous 90 years and the uncivilized tribes were granted ownership of 28% of the land of their territory.

In a prelude to the current contention over most Arctic lands, the discovery of oil off the north coast in 1968 and impact of the civil rights movement and social movements elsewhere in the United States politicized the status of Alaska. The Inupiat Inuit people led a campaign to have their rights to land in the region legally recognized in the face of the huge social and economic changes occurring due to the arrival of oil companies. The 1971 Alaska Native Claims Settlements Act (ANCSA) produced a compromise over this issue and granted ownership of 12% of Alaskan land to native groups by creating regional and village corporations through which they would be guaranteed a slice of future economic development profits. The Arctic Slope Regional Corporation hence became a significant benefactor from the oil boom around Prudhoe Bay. The following year, the North Slope Borough was established, giving significant local government powers to the Inupiat. Taxes raised on oil and gas revenues in the borough have been utilized in schemes advancing indigenous housing, schooling and employment. The Inupiat of the village of Nuiqsut, for example, saw their personal incomes rise by 50% between 1992 and 2002 and local amenities greatly improved from the windfall of having become shareholders in the Arctic Slope Regional Corporation and local Kuukpik Corporation (Caulfield 2004: 132–33). The Northwest Arctic Borough followed suit in 1986 in order to utilize some of the profits from the Red Dog Mine—the world's largest source of zinc.

In a political campaign separate to the indigenous land rights movement, the Alaskan Independence Party (AIP) lobbied for the people of the state to be given the plebiscite on their status not granted in 1959, in line with the UN commitment to decolonization. Led by Joe Vogler, this party at one time openly advocated secession from the Union as the preferred outcome of such a plebiscite.

Box 4.3 Joe Vogler

Figure 4.3 Joe Vogler

Charismatic leader Joe Vogler was born in Kansas but moved to Alaska as a young man, in the course of serving his country during the Second World War, and then settled in Fairbanks as a gold mining entrepreneur. In the 1970s, he founded the Alaskan Independence Party in response to the amount of land requisitioned by the federal government in the construction of the Trans-Alaskan oil pipeline. He disappeared in 1993 shortly before he was due to address the UN on Alaskan independence and was then found to have been murdered. Given that his UN speech had allegedly been funded by the government of Iran, this mysterious incident fuelled inevitable conspiracy theories.

Secession from the United States is no longer an aim held by many in the AIP, but it remains a significant third party in the state campaigning for gun rights and minimal government in line with other American right-wing minority parties.

Tensions between Alaskan indigenous peoples and Washington have also surfaced over environmental policy. In 2011, Alaskan native groups, including the Arctic Slope Regional Corporation and North Slope Borough, sued the federal government over the Polar Bear Cultural Habitat policy restricting economic development in certain areas on the north coast (see Chapter 3) because of the likely consequent loss of revenue that would result. As with many of the Greenlandic Inuit, indigenous rights in Alaska are not about economic isolationism but being able to greet the rest of the world directly rather than going through the federal/colonial capital.

Canada

Canada was from the outset of its independence from Great Britain in 1867 a devolved state, in reflection of its vast size and history of diverse colonial rule by the British and French. Arctic Canada, though, was not initially part of the new Canadian confederation and its later absorption led to these vast tracts of land becoming lesser partners in the emergent federal system. Indeed, in spite of its decolonization from Great Britain, Canada did not decolonize itself until the 1960s, when its northern outposts became part of its federation with their inhabitants gaining the vote in 1962. Although they have gradually acquired greater devolved powers, this legacy persists with federal Canada today consisting of 10 provinces sharing co-sovereign authority with the federal government in Ottawa and three territories across the north with lesser, delegated powers: Northwest Territories, Yukon and Nunavut.

Northwest Territories

The Northwest Territories (NWT) were founded in 1870 as a huge residual mass of land and (from 1880) islands claimed by Canada north of the established provinces. Much of this was ceded by the British-based Hudson Bay Corporation fur-trading business. The legendary Royal Northwest Mounted Police were established in 1873 to assert sovereign control over this wild frontier. The residual character of NWT persists with several border changes, leaving today a diverse and scattered population of 44,000 which is around half aboriginal including sizeable Inuit, Dene (American Indians) and Métis (descended from the intermarriage of American Indians and European settlers) minorities. Territorial status for NWT was merely a geographical convenience until the 1960s, with the federal government in complete control, administering the land from an office in Ottawa. However, in 1967, administrative headquarters were moved to Yellowknife in response to the recommendations of the government-appointed Carrothers Commission, which had highlighted social problems and poor governance in the

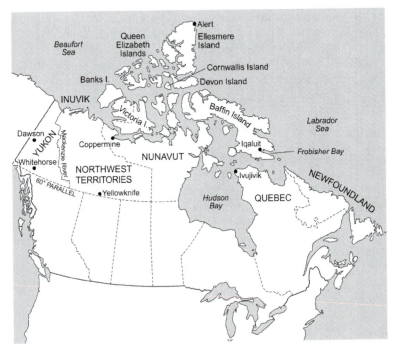

Figure 4.4 Map of Arctic Canada

territory. Although this devolution measure was mainly the result of grievances voiced by non-aboriginal settler communities, indigenous peoples gradually took advantage of the new political reality and, from the 1980s, concluded a series of land claims settlements with the federal government. In 1984, the Committee for the Original People's Entitlement, which had been founded in 1970, secured compensation for the lands and entitlements from future economic activities for the Inuvialuit (Inuit). Similar agreements were concluded by the Gwich'in of the Upper McKenzie delta and the Sahtu Dene and Métis of the Great Bear Lake region in 1992 and 1994, respectively.

Yukon

Yukon Territory was separated from Northwest Territories in 1898 in response to the sudden population increase that resulted from the legendary Klondike gold rush. Native American tribes, although a small minority within the territory, were inspired by the Alaskan Inuit land deal to establish the Council of Yukon First Nations in 1973 to pursue a similar campaign. Twenty years later, the Council secured the first in a series of land claims and self-government agreements, gaining compensation for lands lost nearly a century ago and guaranteeing a slice of future mineral extraction earnings to 14 'First Nation' Indian tribes.

Although there has been some resentment expressed about the more extensive land rights secured by their northern territorial neighbours, Yukon has generally not pushed for greater autonomy than it has, as it lacks their cultural ties, with only one-fifth of its 34,000 population even part-aboriginal.

Nunavut

Nunavut (meaning 'our land') has a much clearer ethnic identity than Yukon or even NWT, having been created as a new federal Territory of Canada in 1999 in the culmination of a campaign for self-determination by the Inuit dating back to 1971. Nunavut is now the largest but least populated Canadian territory, with just 33,000 people, 84% of whom are Inuit. The Inuit had been largely left to their own devices until encroachment into the northeastern parts of Canada increased during the 1950s, when the government sought to modernize and demonstrate sovereignty over their backyard by establishing permanent settlements. Hence, nomadic Inuit were relocated to new towns in the frozen reaches of Ellesmere and Cornwallis Islands (including the world's northernmost settlement Alert), from the relatively temperate climes of northern Quebec, with some dire health and social consequences.

Box 4.4 Timeline of Nunavut home rule

1953–55 Forced relocations of Inuit from northern Quebec to Ellesmere and Cornwallis Islands to strengthen sovereign claims

1969   Federal government appoints a Commissioner of Native Claims in response to heightened grievances voiced by aboriginal groups

1971   Inuit Taprisat of Canada (ITC) formed to articulate aboriginal land rights in the Arctic

1973   Calder v. British Columbia Supreme Court case established principle of an aboriginal title to land predating colonization

1976   ITC present the 'Nunavut proposal' to Ottawa under which Inuit land claims would be ended in exchange for financial compensation and political autonomy

1992   Inuit plebiscite gives 85% support for home rule and a land claims settlement

1993   Canadian parliament passes the Nunavut Act, creating a new territory of the federation (dividing Northwest Territory), and the Nunavut Land Claims Agreement Act giving financial compensation and a share in future profits from economic activities to the Inuit

1999   Nunavut becomes a territory of the Canadian federation on 1 April

---

Unlike in Russia and Alaska, Canada's Arctic indigenous peoples have remained as an ethnic majority in Nunavut which has strengthened their hand. However, despite home rule, lingering legacies of colonialism remain in Nunavut. As analysed in the previous chapter, health standards amongst the indigenous population in the Territory lag far behind most Canadians. The Inuit have the same right to state health provision as other Canadians but often do not seek it because it is invariably delivered by professionals from the south. Since tuberculosis only ever affected these people because of contacts from the south, it is, perhaps, not surprising that such suspicions persist. Hence, Moller concludes that the cure for health problems in Nunavut is decolonization in terms of delivering public health in a manner culturally acceptable to the Inuit and encouraging them to join the health professions themselves (Moller 2010).

Home rule has been a difficult experience and an independent report commissioned by the Territory government concluded of the first decade that, 'without doubt, the expectations most people had of Nunavut at its inception have not been met' (North Sky Consulting Group 2009: 2). In particular, the report highlighted 'dysfunctional elements of the government's internal operating environment', resulting from excessive decentralization which had hampered communication between departments (ibid.: 3).

However, despite widespread dissatisfaction amongst the Inuit with their government, the report also states that 'people everywhere said they supported Nunavut, and remained inspired by the dream that had created it' (ibid.: 1). Nunavut does not possess the raw materials that have fuelled the economic development of Alaskan Inuit and hold the potential to empower Greenlandic and even Russian Inuit. Full independence, consequently, is unthinkable. It does, though, still have the people on its side. Greater autonomy would not necessarily be economically beneficial since being a territory rather than a province entitles them to a greater slice of federal money. Most of the budgets of the three Arctic territories arrives in federal transfers, including some 89% in the case of Nunavut. In reconciling those political holy grails of independence and 'who gets what', more is sometimes less.

Russia: Siberia

Russia's northern fringe has a very long history of resisting control from Moscow and St Petersburg going back to the Tsarist era. A Siberian independence movement was prominent throughout the 19th century and seized the opportunity provided by the Bolshevik revolution to declare a sovereign state in 1918. The rise of the Soviet Union inevitably put paid to any notions of national self-determination with the combined effects of 'Russification' (incentivizing Russian settlement) and enforced urbanization from the 1950s undermining national identities and traditional herding and fishing lifestyles. Subsistence herding and fishing based on the family unit gave way to large collectivized, state-run farms known as *soukhoz*.

In the 1980s, though, the seeds of a revival in localism were sown in the context of Mikhail Gorbachev's policy of restructuring the ailing Soviet economy: perestroika. Devolution, pluralism, greater openness

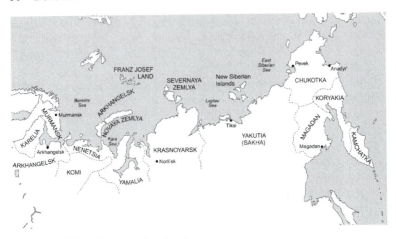

Figure 4.5 Map of the Russian Arctic

(glasnost) and more economic self-reliance (*khosrachet*) were key elements in this new policy which sought to achieve *uskorenie* (speed up economic growth), to reverse the stagnation that had set in after the years of the 'economic miracle' that had seen the Soviet Union emerge as a superpower. The hope was that growth would be stimulated by relaxing central control and so giving producers a limited means of making personal profits as an incentive for greater production. It was also considered that *uskorenie* could be aided by permitting greater freedom of expression in order to expose where there was complacency in local administration and producing constructive criticism of the overall political system. Although perestroika became the prelude to the break-up of the Soviet Union in 1991, it is important to remember that Gorbachev's support for devolution and willingness to abandon the Soviet empire in Eastern Europe and Afghanistan was not a liberalist green light for non-Russian secessionists within his country. The brutal suppression of Lithuanian independence in 1990 is evidence of this. Gorbachev sought to modernize his multinational country and its governing ideology rather than abandon them. Devolution was an act of pragmatism not liberal nationalism. Empowering the far-flung regions of his vast country with more autonomy and self-reliance would cut the costs of subsidizing them from the centre. Decentralization in this way can simultaneously serve the interests of both core and peripheries.

In the context of the newly emerging political atmosphere in Gorbachev's USSR, the journal of the Soviet Communist Party, *Kommunist*, in 1988 published a landmark article by anthropologists Pika and Prokhorov,

'The Big Problems of the Small Peoples', which highlighted the social and economic marginalization of the indigenous population of the north and called for them to be given political representation. They observed frankly that 'Living Standards are much lower for the indigenous Northerners than for the immigrant population', citing explanatory factors that included a record decline in reindeer numbers and the social dislocation resulting from children being taken to boarding schools far away from their homes (Pika and Prokhorov 1988: 76). Pika became a pivotal figure linking the Russian academics to emergent indigenous leaders and also with the international community, through the International Work Group for Indigenous Affairs (IWGIA). IWGIA, a group of anthropologists established in 1968 initially to highlight the plight of South American Indians, published an English version of 'The Big Problems of the Small Peoples' and then set up a Moscow office with Pika as a board member (Dahl 2009: 63–64).

Grassroots activism accompanied this intellectual renaissance with most initial focus on the impact of the oil industry on reindeer herding in Yamal. The group Yamal for the Future Generations was formed by the Nenets of that province in 1988 and, in the following year, the Rescue of the Iugra was launched in Khanit-Manis, along with the broader Association of Numerically Small Peoples of the North. The Sakhar Republic was the most dramatically affected with a series of demonstrations and strikes and some ethnic clashes between the Sakhar and Russians, such as the 1987 Yakutsk State University riots (Balzer and Vimokurova 1996).

Gorbachev rode this wave of indigenous empowerment and launched the Russian Association of Indigenous Peoples of the North, Siberia and Far East (RAIPON) at a 1990 Congress at the Kremlin. RAIPON today is an umbrella association of the 41 recognized ethnic groups of northern Russia, constituting around 250,000 people. They host a Congress every four years to discuss issues of specific concern to these communities and channel funds to projects and encourage the production of publications concerning indigenous rights. RAIPON is the chief international mouthpiece of Russia's northern indigenous peoples with non-governmental organization (NGO) representation at the Arctic Council and consultative status with the UN via the Economic and Social Council (ECOSOC).

In 1990, Boris Yeltsin, the president of a Russia acting much like a sovereign entity ahead of its formal independence in 1991, looked to trump Gorbachev over devolution and court the support of the minority nationalities of his Soviet Socialist Republic by announcing that they could 'take as much autonomy as they can swallow'. The Sakha

Republic, Kareliya, Chukotka and Yamalo-Nenetski consequently declared their 'sovereignty' (autonomy but not full independence) in September 1990, with some of their emergent nationalist politicians and parties becoming key allies of Yeltsin in his battle for Russian secession from the USSR. Mikhail Nikolayev, for example, graduated from being Chairman of the Supreme Soviet to become Sakha's first president for his backing of Yeltsin (Kempton and Clark 2002: 77). Following the dissolution of the USSR in 1991, when the 15 Soviet Socialist Republics that constituted this highly centralized Union became new, independent states, this manifested itself in the codification of a new Constitution for the Russian Federation in 1993. Article 69 of the Constitution highlighted the desire of the new Russian state to appease Western liberals by stating a guarantee of the political rights of indigenous people in line with international law. The new Russian parliament (Duma) was similarly decentralized with half of its membership made up of regional representatives who, from 1996, were directly elected (the other half made up of politicians from cross-Russian party lists). In this context, Sakha negotiated the right to secede in their Republic Constitution. Whilst Yeltsin's willingness to go to war to suppress Chechen separatism proved that he was not prepared to allow the minority nations to 'chew' on full independence, Russia nonetheless underwent a significant devolution of power in the 1990s.

The autonomous *okrugs* are unique to the Arctic region, intended to reflect the particular circumstances of some of the northern indigenous peoples. These are, however, no more ethnically homogenous than the other federal units due to Soviet-era Russification and post-Soviet influxes of workers to the oil and gas fields. Only 5% of Yamalo-Nenets' population are of the titular nationality (i.e. Nenets), far outnumbered by Russians and even Ukrainian migrant oil workers. In Sakha Republic, the titular nationality (the Yakuts), who are Turkic people, have tended to be at the forefront of Siberian autonomy movements owing to the economic muscle provided by being host to nearly all of Russia's diamonds.

Yeltsin's rapid post-communist transition plan, which entailed a radical embrace of privatization and the mass sale of state-owned industries in the early 1990s, had profound effects on Arctic Russia. In 1992, a law was passed to recreate pre-soviet-style communes (*obschiny*) to take the place of the state-run collective farms (*sovkhoz*) set up to modernize subsistence and small-scale agriculture from the 1920s. The word *obschina* was deliberately chosen to mark the re-establishment of traditional family clan holdings in place of the huge farms run by government appointees that had been created from merging such holdings. However, the original *obschiny* predated both communism and capitalism in Russia and in the context of private industry and land ownership represent a quite different proposition to the romanticized notion of a return to traditional lifestyles for the Russian Inuit and other northern indigenous peoples. 'By formalizing ownership of territory and assigning the property to sets of individuals, the family/clan holding is generally oriented toward the market' (Ziker 2002: 299).

Stammler views the new *obschiny* not as a means of empowering the small-numbered peoples but as a new tool to reassert control from Moscow (Stammler 2005). The Bartels are also critical, seeing the development as a backward step since, in their view, they 'exacerbate threats to Northerners' traditional lands and resources and erode the benefits that most Soviet citizens enjoyed such as state-sponsored food, housing, transport, day care, health care, guaranteed jobs et cetera' (Bartels and Bartels 2006: 274). Indeed, herding has actually become harder in the capitalist era since much of this was able to persist unofficially in the era of collectivization. For many small-scale agriculturalists in the Russian north, private ownership has proven more restrictive than centralized absolutist rule.

Under the presidency of Vladimir Putin, 2000–08, there was a notable re-centralization of Russia, prompted both by the continuation of armed separatism in the Caucasus and a concern that decentralization had actually worsened local administration. The horrific 2004 Beslan School massacre by Chechen terrorists provided the catalyst for the Russian political system to be 'radically restructured in order to strengthen the unity of the country and prevent further crises' (speech by Putin in Moscow, 13 September 2004, quoted in Baker 2004: A01). Elected officials were replaced by Kremlin appointees and seven federal supervisors were created to tighten Moscow's control of the now notionally federal units.

Research by Hagendoorn *et al.* has estimated that 40% of the titular (though minority) nationality in Karelia and 53% of the Yakuts in Sakha supported independence from Russia, whether individually or in some form of regional association (Hagendoorn *et al.* 2008). This support for separatism, though, is as much about economic pragmatism as ethnic consciousness since the research also suggests that nearly a third of Russians in the two republics also support separatism. This mirrors the independence movements in some of the Soviet Socialist Republics in the early 1990s when most Russians in the Ukraine, Latvia and Belarus voted in plebiscites for secession from Russia, alongside the more conventional 'nationalists'. This was also somewhat comparable to the settler-based Alaskan independence movement.

Notably in 2010, in a display of growing antipathy with domination from Moscow, many northern residents not covered by the existing titular nationalities identified themselves as the self-defined category of 'Sibiryak' on the census forms completed that year.

As with the Russian Federation overall, an initial apparent embrace of bottom-up democratic devolution in Siberia in the early 1990s has given way to a more top-down bureaucratic structure in RAIPON and led some to suggest that the association is more of a forum for allocating business contracts in the north run from a Moscow office (Rethmann 2004). However, whilst RAIPON might not be an independent, grassroots NGO comparable to the indigenous movements in North America, it has been able to offer something of a centrifugal counter to Putin's centralization. The sheer existence of RAIPON and the 1993 Constitution, particularly on the international stage, ensures that the genie is out of the bottle and able to grant some, albeit limited, native wishes. The ICC and Danish government have allocated funding to RAIPON's Moscow office and subsidized the production of events and materials advancing indigenous rights. Between 2000 and 2002, three federal laws concerning northern indigenous peoples were enacted after RAIPON campaigns, dealing with rights, natural resources and community organization.[1] Of course, these laws have not heralded the transformation of Russia into a multi-cultural consociationalist democracy but RAIPON's presence at Arctic and global intergovernmental and non-governmental forums allows it to hold the Kremlin to account and secure some victories against the carve-up of Siberia. Moscow has persisted with several controversial initiatives, such as the construction of the Yakutia-Khabarovsk gas pipeline, without consulting local opinion, and creating bureaucratic obstacles that restrict traditional fishing, but RAIPON has still spearheaded some significant initiatives. In 2010, their campaign succeeded in postponing the construction of a dam and hydroelectric power station on the Lower Tunguska River in Krasnoyarsk because it would have entailed the relocation of many Evenk people (Wessendorf 2011). That RAIPON is no Kremlin poodle is evident from considering the stinging rebukes they have conferred on their government through the exposure provided by their role within the UN.

> Indigenous people have become more vulnerable due to the failure to implement laws, which would afford a bare minimum of protection to land and resource use rights. At the same time, Russia has enacted new laws and regulations that serve to undermine indigenous people's subsistence rights, restrict their access to sources of food and income and allow their territories to be put under the

control of third parties and therefore must be considered retrogressive measures.

(RAIPON/IWGIA 2011: 26)

The free expression of these words by a Russian NGO to the political world does not correspond with the overall impression of the giant country's retreat from democratization and decentralization and illustrates how globalization can sustain these ideas even in the face of a powerful government. The people of the Russian north may be 'small numbered' but they are now well known to the rest of the political world and active on that stage. The *obschiny* may have undermined traditional livelihoods but they have also helped forge national identities through the literal construction of 'self and other' in the region. The Kremlin cannot simply ignore their northern folk. They have an economic incentive to keep them on board and must also contend with the bald truth that Russia is simply too big a country to be run exclusively from Muscovite offices.

Arctic peoples, globalization and the redefining of sovereignty

Whilst the cold wave of self-determination sweeping across the territories of the Arctic bears some comparison with previous waves of decolonization and more recent 'peripheral nationalist' (Hechter 2000) movements within sovereign states, a striking difference is that the campaigns reviewed in this chapter are very much 21st-century phenomena, consciously working within the parameters of a globalizing world in which the meaning of sovereignty is changing. This was expressed eloquently in the 2009 ICC's 'Declaration of Sovereignty':

> sovereignty is a contested concept, however, and does not have a fixed meaning. Old ideas of sovereignty are breaking down as different governance models, such as the European Union, evolve.

(ICC 2009)

The declaration predictably trumpets a 'right to self-determination in the Arctic' and that 'states are obligated to respect and promote the realization of our right to self-determination', but also makes it plain that 'Inuit are citizens of Arctic states', with the rights and responsibilities that this carries (ICC 2009).

Paradoxically, globalization, whilst threatening the indigenous peoples of the High North, also serves to enhance their standing in the world. The implications of globalization for sovereignty throughout the world play into the hands of an Inuit or Sami interpretation of political autonomy. Whilst established sovereign states struggle to cope with diminishing autonomy and control over their territory, money and populations, Arctic people see their traditional looser and less territorially based claims to autonomy become more normalized and more realizable.

Whilst, as outlined in the previous chapter, globalization is wreaking havoc in the far north in terms of the environmental and social changes it is unleashing, the globalization of ideas increasingly provides a discourse and platform for the articulation of the values of Inuit, Sami and other indigenous Arctic peoples. Devolution has become increasingly the norm in state administration through much of the world, as limits to sovereign control have slowly become apparent to governments. This, predictably, is most apparent in liberal democracies but is also evident in more authoritarian political systems, such as Russia's. Governing far-flung and thinly populated territories, which in relative terms Arctic lands will remain in spite of the thaw, is a costly business and made easier if it is with the broad consent of the people who live there. The people of the Arctic have, in general, recognized this and are able to use it to their advantage.

As discussed in Chapter 2, the Arctic powers need their northern folk onside in order to be able to project and reinforce their sovereign claims in the region. The people of the north are able to use this as a bargaining chip to secure more rights and autonomy, whilst recognizing that their own full sovereign independence may be too much of a gamble. Globalization can be tamed by working with it. In a case of 'What does not kill you makes you stronger', the acute threats posed by globalization strengthen the political hand of northern peoples since these are threats shared by the rest of the world, albeit usually to a lesser extent. The plight of Arctic people exemplifies the general fears engendered by globalization but their response to such threats emphasize how the ill effects of global change are best remedied by working with rather than futilely opposing global forces. Hence, Arctic peoples have themselves embraced, and also come to epitomize, the need for global citizenship. The Sami and particularly the Inuit have actively contributed to the evolving global discourse which is slowly empowering individuals and indigenous peoples and moving us away from a purely state-centric world. Hence, the need for indigenous rights, the 'right to health' and environmentally sustainable living are both exemplified and articulated by the people of the Arctic.

The Arctic's indigenous population is, in general, an arch exponent of sustainable development and the notion of the stewardship—rather than the possession—of land (Shadian 2010). The key catalyst for advances in Sami self-determination was the fact that their resistance to the pursuit of profit over people and traditional advocacy of localized self-sufficiency chimed with an emergent ecological movement. The Inuit and environmental international NGOs have not always made the most comfortable of bedfellows, given the resentment felt by the former against the promotion of restriction on traditional hunting practices, but the traditional lifestyles of these people also represent a model for sustainable development and appreciating humanity's place in the natural world. Similarly, the people of the High North have also come to be heard speaking the words of human rights and particularly indigenous rights, as enshrined in the 2007 UN Declaration on the Rights of Indigenous Peoples.

The ICC's reference to the EU in their declaration of sovereignty is telling. International Relations theories had traditionally been divided into two predictable camps by the Western European integration phenomenon: Liberals believing that state sovereignty was being superseded by the onset of a United States of Europe (either rapidly, for Federalists, or gradually, for Neo-functionalists); and neo-Realists who saw cooperation as set to go no further than satisfying mutual trading interests with national interests ensuring that monetary and foreign policy would continue to be determined locally. From the 1990s, though, the continuation of integrative ventures, such as the single currency, alongside the persistence of states seeing such change as being in their own interests, prompted a reappraisal of thinking in line with the simultaneous rise of Social Constructivist thought coming to influence the discipline. The notion of 'dual sovereignty', in which political authority is shared between the national and supranational level through mutual interest, has since become mainstream thinking. Many EU analysts have come to embrace approaches such as consociationalism, which abandons the notion of choosing between integration and sovereignty, seeing the two as not mutually exclusive and even enjoying a mutually reinforcing symbiotic relationship. 'The merging of distinct politically organised states in some form of union to further common ends without losing either national identity or resigning individual sovereignty' (Chryssochoou 2007: 365). The states of the EU will continue to work towards an 'ever closer union', not on the assumption that this is eroding their sovereignty and influence but through the realization that this is the best way to preserve these attributes in a globalizing world. Sub-state nationalist movements, such as the Scots, northern Italians and (moderate) Basques, have generally bought into this idea alongside the member states of the EU, in what Anthony Smith has termed 'moderate nationalism' (Smith

1995: 147–59). The Scottish National Party's election slogan of 'an independent Scotland within Europe', launched in 1988 and revived periodically since then, has often been derided by Eurosceptic critics as oxymoronic given the extent of EU authority. However, the desire to have a direct line to Brussels whilst accepting that a proportion of political authority will come from there has struck many others as a pragmatic and realistic response to a changing economic world in which traditional autonomy is simply no longer an option. The EU is unique and not directly analogous to international political cooperation in the Arctic, but the Sami and Inuit are conscious that they have a stronger role in the Arctic Council than non-Arctic observers and, hence, confer their support on this more classically intergovernmental organization.

For the people of the Arctic, sovereignty is defined more in external than internal terms, granting them the ability to conclude international agreements and contribute to global political discourse. Even the Russian Inuit have found a role in the world thanks to support from other Inuit and the establishment of links to international organizations. Also, these are sovereign claims not based on the notion of exclusivity of control of land in line with (traditional) Sami and Inuit culture of common ownership and grazing. Far from romanticizing the 'primitive' knowledge of the traditional hunter-gatherer, however, this represents a postmodern, cutting-edge appreciation of the limits and realities of sovereignty in the 21st century.

As asserted by Zellen, this collision between absolutist Westphalian sovereignty and common land ownership represents a 'Clash of the Civilizations' actually more profound than the supposed Western–Islamic confrontation (Zellen 2010: 21). Al-Qaeda and the West each want to assert control of land and resources vis-à-vis each other but are not disputing the whole concept of land ownership. It is a clash seen many times in the history of domestic politics, from 'The Enclosures' of 17th-century England, to the collectivization of communism, to the development of countries of the 'Third World', but not one that has ever really manifested itself on the international political stage. Additionally, despite similar asymmetries of power to such earlier struggles, it is not inevitable that the political model to emerge from this dialectic will further advance private or state land ownership over common stewardship. Governments are coming to terms, albeit slowly, with the limits of their powers and embracing internal and external compromises on their sovereignty in order to survive and prosper in a globalizing world. Due to a wind of change fanned not only by the colonized but also by their colonizers, the Arctic may well emerge as a region pioneering the ICC's vision of 'multi-level governance systems' in place of the traditional monopoly claimed by states in the area of foreign affairs (ICC 2009).

Note

1 'On the Guarantee of the Rights of the Numerically Small Indigenous People of the North 2000'; On Traditional Natural Resource Use of Indigenous Numerically Small People of the North 2001'; and On Basic Principles of Organizing Communities of Indigenous People of the North, Siberia and Far East 2002'.

5 Intergovernmental cooperation
The top table

Box 5.1 Gorbachev's Murmansk speech, 1987

Figure 5.1 Mikhail Gorbachev

On 1 October 1987, Soviet President Mikhail Gorbachev launched the 'Murmansk Initiative' with a landmark speech appealing to the West to join him in transforming the Arctic into a 'zone of peace and fruitful cooperation' (Gorbachev 1987). The initiative can be understood in the wider context of Gorbachev's desire to end the Cold War and usher in a new era of accommodation with the West. The Arctic, on the fault line between East and West but not at its epicentre, was seen as a testing ground for this new, more cooperative political world. The key themes referred to in the Murmansk address included:

- Denuclearization
- Naval arms control
- Confidence-building measures
- Energy cooperation

- Scientific cooperation
- Empowerment of indigenous peoples
- Environmental cooperation
- Opportunities from the opening of the Northern Sea Route.

Introduction

With the exception of naval arms control, where nonetheless tensions have eased, international cooperation has grown in all of these areas since then to an extent barely conceivable in the mid-1980s. This chapter will explore how this intergovernmental cooperation has developed since then with particular emphasis on the Arctic Council (AC), the seed of which was sown at Murmansk.

Intergovernmental organizations and international regimes in the Arctic

That Murmansk was a catalyst for a growth in intergovernmental politics is beyond dispute but some previous cross-border political initiatives also used the Arctic as a testing ground for pioneering cooperation. As highlighted in previous chapters, the Polar Bear Treaty was able to cross the Cold War divide and emerge in the era of détente in the 1970s, and both sides of the Iron Curtain also co-existed as a consequence of the Svalbard Treaty dating back to 1920. Going back even further, the North Pacific Fur Seal Convention of 1911 brought together the great powers of Great Britain (representing Canada), the United States, Russia and Japan in a short-lived but pioneering and successful conservation regime in the Bering Sea (Young and Osherenko 1993: 29–34).

Though the term was not employed at the time, the polar bear and fur seal arrangements were/are *international regimes* rather than intergovernmental organizations. International regime is a broader definition of international cooperation which came to prominence in the 1980s as representing 'implicit or explicit principles, norms, rules and decision-making procedures around which actors' expectations converge in a given area of international relations' (Krasner 1983: 1). An intergovernmental organization (IGO) is a more formalized form of cross-border cooperation (or regime), characterized as involving explicit rules and a clearly defined decision-making process. Hence, an IGO is more than a treaty, although they are often established as the result of one. An IGO has a 'life of its own' in that it is intended to be permanent and to evolve according to changing circumstances. It will have a fixed headquarters staffed by its own secretariat and some form of policy-making process by which new binding rules can be developed as and when required by its member states. Until very recently, intergovernmental cooperation in the Arctic was purely of the less formal kind, but the Arctic Council has now evolved into a fully fledged IGO and governance in the region today is centred on this institution in addition to several looser regimes.

The Arctic Council

The Arctic Council evolved from the 1991 Arctic Environmental Protection Strategy (AEPS), but the idea of a permanent institution for the Arctic was around at the same time that this regime was being developed at the end of the 1980s. Following up on the Murmansk initiative, the Finnish government initiated discussions on an environmental treaty for the Arctic, culminating in this then being signed by the eight Arctic states at a Rovaniemi ministerial conference in 1991. This particular proposal was informal with no commitment to institution-building but, at the same time, with the stated aim to 'identify, reduce, and as a final goal, eliminate pollution' (AEPS 1991: 2), was ambitious. The AEPS committed the eight to an Action Plan promoting scientific cooperation and the carrying out of environmental impact assessments for industrial projects in the region. This and further forms of environmental cooperation would be conducted primarily through regular meetings of four working groups: the Arctic Monitoring and Assessment Programme (AMAP); Protection of Arctic Marine Environment (PAME); Emergency Prevention, Preparedness and Response (EPPR); and Conservation of Arctic Flora and Fauna (CAFF).

In 1989, simultaneous to the talks leading up to the AEPS, Canadian Prime Minister Brian Mulroney at a Leningrad bilateral meeting proposed 'a council of Arctic countries eventually coming into existence to coordinate and promote cooperation' (Rothwell 1996: 243). The Canadian State Department then worked on developing such a proposal and put it forward at the Rovaniemi ministerial whilst AEPS was being formalized. Mulroney's proposal, seemingly, was an unscripted and spontaneous conciliatory gesture influenced by drawing on recent academic proposals of the Canadian Institute of International Affairs Cooperation (Nord 2006: 297; Rothwell 1996: 243). In 1992, after the fall of the Soviet Union, an Arctic intergovernmental forum was then officially endorsed when President Yeltsin and Mulroney met in Ottawa to sign the Canadian-Russian Declaration of Friendship and Cooperation (Nord 2006: 300). The Canadians also secured the endorsement of the Nordic states and the Inuit Circumpolar Conference (ICC) for the plan. The US George Bush (Sr) Administration, though, was ambivalent to the idea, fearful of anything that restricted their military hand and still operating in a culture of Realist mistrust of international organizations despite having come to play a more constructive role in the United Nations (UN) than had been the case in the 1980s. The greater trust in multilateralism under the Bill Clinton presidency, though, saw US endorsement for an Arctic forum secured in 1995, but with the proviso that military issues be off limits and the new body be strictly informal (Hasanda 2009).

International regimes in the Arctic developed significantly in the early 1990s prior to the launch of the Arctic Council. In 1993, the Nuuk Declaration on Environment and Development added the Task Force on Sustainable Development and Utilization to the AEPS roster, whilst the Canadians continued to pursue a wider and more formal Arctic polity. That year also saw the first Conference of Parliamentarians of the Arctic 8 in Reykjavik which, when then convened, promptly gave its support for an Arctic Council. That conference then spawned the Standing Committee (SCPAR) the following year to coordinate business in between subsequent conferences every few months in different Arctic countries. SCPAR has hence become a 'shadow Arctic Council'—an informal gathering of parliamentarians of the 'Arctic 8' ('A8') plus members of the European Parliament and representatives of indigenous peoples, which meets every two years.

In 1996, the Ottawa Declaration launched the Arctic Council building on AEPS by adding a commitment to 'common issues' other than environmental ones (apart from military matters). Two years later, AEPS was formally absorbed into the AC and the organization's Rules of Procedure were adopted. The five AEPS working groups were retained but with the intention of adding a sixth group on Arctic contaminants, which was initially set up as a steering committee and action plan. All working groups contain representatives of the A8 governments and the 'Permanent Participants' representing indigenous peoples.

The AC Chair rotates between the Arctic 8 every two years accompanied by a biennial ministerial at which decisions are taken by the consensus of the A8 (i.e. unanimity). In addition, 'senior Arctic officials' (SAOs) meet every six months in the country holding the presidency to flesh out ministerial strategy. SAOs take reports from the A8 or permanent participants to work on and prepare recommendations for the ministerials as well as acting on issues delegated to them by the biennial summits. SAOs also coordinate the work of the working groups and any other ad hoc groups or task forces.

In addition to the eight member states, the AC is notable for opening its doors to a large number of other participants and observers. Representatives of six transnational indigenous peoples are recognized with the right to attend all meetings and submit reports, though not be included in the decision-making process. These Permanent Participants are: the Aleut International Association; Arctic Athabaskan Council; Gwich'in Council International; ICC; Sami Council; and the Russian Association of Indigenous Peoples of the North, Siberia and Far East (RAIPON).

Six non-Arctic states have been recognized from the start as permanent observers: the UK, France, Germany, Netherlands, Poland and Spain. Government representatives of these states have no voting rights but are able to submit statements at ministerial meetings and propose agenda items. China, Japan, South Korea, Italy and the European Union (EU) have been included as observers on an ad hoc basis since 2008–09, but none was able to secure agreement on making this permanent at the 2009 and 2011 ministerials. Also with observer status are the following intergovernmental organizations/regimes: SCPAR; Nordic Council; Nordic Environmental Finance Corporation; International Union for the Conservation of Nature; UN Economic Commission for Europe; UN Environment Programme (UNEP); UN Development Programme (UNDP); International Federation of Red Cross and Red Crescent Societies (IFRC); and North Atlantic Marine Mammal Commission. Additionally, the following non-governmental organizations (NGOs) have observer status: the International Arctic Science Committee; International Arctic Social Sciences Association (IASSA); Northern Forum; Advisory Committee on the Protection of the Seas; Arctic Circumpolar Gateway; Circumpolar Conservation Union; International Union for Circumpolar Health; International Working Group for Indigenous Affairs (IWGIA); University of the Arctic; and WWF.

The 2011 Nuuk ministerial marked a watershed, with agreements reached to establish a permanent secretariat and ratify the organization's first legally binding agreement—the 2011 'Agreement on Cooperation on Aeronautical and Maritime Search and Rescue in the Arctic'. This enhanced status for the AC was clearly illustrated by the attendance of Hillary Clinton at the summit, becoming the first US Secretary of State to attend, with Secretary of the Interior Ken Salazar also brought

Table 5.1 Chronology of the Arctic Council

Chair	Declaration	Key developments
	Ottawa 1996	AMAP mandated to produce report on the State of the Arctic Environment
Canada 1996–98	Iqaluit 1998	PAME mandated to work on a maritime safety Polar Code with the International Maritime Organization
United States 1998–2000	Barrow 2000	Adopted Sustainable Development Framework document
Finland 2000–02	Inari 2002	Agreed on an action plan and projects to implement the Sustainable Development Programme
Iceland 2002–04	Reykjavik 2004	AMAP mandated to complete assessments on oil and gas impacts
Russia 2004–06	Salekhard 2006	Arctic Contaminants Working Group formally recognized
Norway 2006–09	Tromsø 2009	Approved the Arctic Marine Shipping Assessment
Denmark 2009–11	Nuuk 2011	Permanent Secretariat agreed. Binding Search and Rescue agreement
Sweden 2011–13	Kiruna 2013	
Canada 2013–15		

along. The AC, hence, has been transformed from a 'high-level forum', as described at the Ottawa Declaration, to a fully fledged intergovernmental organization with a permanent base and binding rules emanating from a decision-making process.

A permanent secretariat in Tromsø was put into practice the year following the Nuuk Declaration. This was a straightforward transition since the venue had been functioning as an unofficial secretariat for several years after being maintained by the Danes and Swedes during their Chairing after Norway had used it. This was reminiscent of the 'troika' system used in the EU to smooth the changeovers in presidency and is a practice that the Nordic states have employed in a range of international diplomatic settings. The permanent secretariat, in line with other IGOs, was to handle day-to-day administration and have a director appointed (for a four-year term with the possibility of being renewed once) as a lead individual to represent the AC internationally. Some 42.5% of the secretariat budget (of initially just under US$1.75 million per year) is provided by the Norwegian government (Arctic Council 2012).

The search and rescue (SAR) agreement was initiated at the 2009 Tromsø ministerial which set up a task force co-chaired by the United States and Russia. The co-chairs convened five meetings to flesh out the rules of the regime which bind the A8 to lead search and rescue missions for ships in distress of any nationality in their ascribed zone of the Arctic Ocean and seas. Information exchange and joint safety training is also ensured in the Treaty as well as a commitment to attend future meetings, at which new requirements may be agreed. The SAR agreement is modelled on the 1944 Convention on International Civil Aviation and 1979 International Convention on Maritime Search and Rescue. At the same time as launching the first binding treaty, the 2011 Nuuk ministerial also may have initiated the second by setting up a task force to prepare an instrument on Arctic Marine Oil Pollution Preparedness and Response (AMOPPR), which was to be considered at the 2013 ministerial. The ministerial did not indicate that this would be a legally binding agreement but such terminology emerged in the meetings of the task force and meetings of the AC SAOs in 2012. Again, AMOPPR is a strengthened regional application of a global treaty, the 1990 International Convention on Oil Pollution Preparedness, Response and Cooperation. Hence, a trend can be seen whereby the Arctic 8 governments are not so much creating regional international law as coming gradually to adopt and nurture existing rules.

Whilst military security matters remain outside the remit of the AC, a seed of intergovernmental cooperation has been sown. Military chiefs of staff of the A8 met for the first time in Newfoundland in 2012, where it was announced that these meetings would become annual events cooperating in the provision of military support for civil emergencies, building on the AC Search and Rescue agreement. Again, this is somewhat reminiscent of the EU where informal cooperation has grown as a spin-off of more formal integration in less sensitive political areas.

Before the launch of its first hard law policy, though, it is clear that the AC had been responsible for a steady growth of *soft law* agreements, lacking official legal rigour but nonetheless having a political impact. The United States and Russia, fearful of extra burdens on their oil and gas industries, were initially lukewarm on involving themselves in AC oil and gas assessments but were gradually brought on board and came to contribute greatly to them (Stokke and Honneland 2007: 176–77). The 'softness' of environmental and maritime safety issues is, in fact, the key to their significance in Arctic intergovernmental politics. The United States and Russia are prepared to work collaboratively on these less sensitive issues in the AC in ways they have often been reluctant to do on the global stage. Hence, at the same time as presidents of the United States and Russia have sometimes been in denial about climate change, their administrations have put their names to the Arctic Climate Impact Assessment (ACIA) and numerous ministerial statements that have done much to advance global policy on this issue.

There is no doubt that indigenous peoples have been empowered by their visible presence in the AC. It has enhanced the profile of the ICC and Sami Council, whilst the Arctic Athabaskan Council and Gwich'in Council were formed specifically in response to opportunities offered by AC representation (Stokke and Honneland 2007: 175). The trend has been set for not excluding indigenous group applicants as long as they meet the criteria of representing indigenous peoples of more than one country.[1] This dimension of the AC adds to its external credibility as representing the people of the world amongst the most affected by climate change rather than just representing a cabal of states actually largely responsible for the problem and likely to exacerbate it by mutually despoiling the Arctic.

The existence of the AC has also assisted in making the region more visible on the global political stage and influencing international policy in a wider sense. Climate change and persistent organic pollutants (POPs) assessments from AC working groups have fed into the global regimes in those areas, as is particularly evidenced by the Intergovernmental Panel on Climate Change's 2007 Assessment Report featuring a chapter specific to the Arctic (Stokke and Honneland 2007: 78–138). The AC has become the chief source of both regional governance and regional representation on the global stage.

Northern Forum

Launched in 1991 as part of the same post-Murmansk momentum that led to the Arctic Council, the Northern Forum (NF), whilst somewhat left in the shade by that organization, nonetheless persists as a distinctive political talking shop for the same region and beyond into neighbouring northern seas. The idea of such a forum was actually advanced as far back as 1974 by the governor of the northernmost Japanese island of Hokkaido, Naohiro Dougakinai, on hosting the first International Conference on Human Development in Northern Regions, attended by regional representatives from Canada, the United States, Norway, Sweden and Finland.

Dougakinai's vision was able to take shape with the Cold War thaw, which saw a Northern Regions Conference set up in 1990 in Anchorage with fourteen regional governments of seven states: Russia, Canada, the United States, Iceland, Japan, China and South Korea. A first General Assembly was then held at Tromsø in 1993 and they have occurred biennially since then with a 20th anniversary meeting in Pyeongchang, South Korea, in 2011. The NF serves as a vehicle for sub-national politicians of resource-rich countries to share knowledge on how to negotiate effectively with their national governments. It supports local events and policies that promote sustainable development, health and indigenous rights in remote northern regions. In particular, the NF has come to be something of a business forum—with some companies given observer status—giving it some distinctiveness over the Arctic Council and also, perhaps, some helpful complementarity (Young 2002). Much NF work has focused on infrastructural projects promoting civil aviation and the use of the Northern Sea Route.

The NF Secretariat was switched from Anchorage to Yakutsk in 2012, which had previously acted as a regional sub-secretariat, reflecting an increasing Russian flavour to the Forum. There is no doubt that the NF has been overshadowed by the AC, with its membership having halved from what it was in the 1990s. Most NF dropouts are from North America, since their domestic political autonomy and clout make an international forum facilitating this superfluous to their needs. Russian northern outposts though, lacking the autonomy of Alaska or the Canadian territories, have seen it as a useful vehicle for demonstrating solidarity against a centralizing Moscow.

Barents Euro-Arctic Region (BEAR)

The BEAR is a unique, multi-layered international regime established by a Norwegian initiative with the 1993 Kirkenes Declaration, launching the intergovernmental Barents Euro-Arctic Council (BEAC) and inter-regional Barents Regional Council. Finland, Norway, Russia and Sweden are the 'core member states' of BEAC, which additionally includes Denmark, Iceland and the EU. There is indigenous representation for three groups—the Sami, Nenets and Veps—whilst the UK, United States, Poland, Netherlands, Japan, Italy, Germany and Canada have observer status. Like the AC, the BEAR also explicitly excludes military matters and it pledges to avoid duplicating work of other forums, declaring its remit to be 'cohesion, good governance and sustainable growth' (BEAR 2012). Ministerial meetings are held biannually and a Committee of Senior Officials meets four times per year. Ten years on from the BEAR's inauguration, the Kirkenes Declaration of 2003 highlighted sustainable development, environmental protection, social development and customs/police/border control cooperation as its priority issues. Health has also emerged as an important area of BEAR activity, as was apparent in the establishment of the Barents HIV programme in 2005.

BEAC is chaired on a two-yearly basis rotated between the core members. As with the Arctic Council, Nordic cooperation has advanced the case for an official headquarters and secretariat. Originally, the four core members used their own designated secretariats but the Norwegian one, at Kirkenes, has always been the largest and has emerged as the unofficial home to the organization and wider regime.

The Barents Regional Council (BRC) is a parallel development to BEAC, bringing together 13 sub-state regions and several indigenous groups in a wider, looser arrangement.[2] The BRC has sought to promote economic growth in the region through initiatives such as the development of east–west transport links to accompany the south–north-focused network and measures to mitigate against youth migration out of the region.

In a third layer, the Parliamentary Barents Conferences have brought together members of parliament and sub-national representatives since 1997.

Northern Dimension

The Northern Dimension (ND) idea was initiated by the Finnish government in 1997, two years after their admission to the EU, and then promoted during their first stint in the presidency in 1999. In a manner similar to Nordic 'troika' cooperation in the AC and the BEAR, this was then followed up by Sweden and Denmark in their presidencies in 2001 and 2002. The EU, Iceland, Norway and Russia are the four members of the ND coming together in biennial foreign ministerials with deputy meetings in the intervening years and steering group meetings three times per year.

The ND was, at first, 'vague' (Stokke and Honneland 2007: 5), but has come to acquire some clout through utilizing several existing EU financial instruments. These include: the Technical Assistance for the Commonwealth of Independent States (TACIS) fund, which is targeted at Russia; the Poland, Hungary: Aid for Restructuring of the Economies (PHARE), which directed aid to other Central/Eastern European post-communist states; and Interreg, which promotes cross-border cooperation within the EU. TACIS has been particularly significant in giving the EU a remit to act on nuclear safety issues in the Russian Arctic, since a key catalyst for this instrument was a European desire to help avoid a repetition of the 1986 Chernobyl disaster. Hence, one of the ND's most notable achievements has been to help fund nuclear waste disposal and security measures at the Gremikha naval base on the Kola Peninsula. Overall, ND work has progressed through partnerships in the environment, public health and social well-being, transport and logistics, and culture—all of which were renewed in 2006.

The 'A5'

As previously discussed, there has been much speculation, and concern amongst some, that the Arctic Council could come to be superseded by a more exclusive 'Arctic 5' club born of the 2008 Ilulissat meeting. This summit was instigated by Danish Foreign Minister Per Stig Möller to discuss issues of Arctic Ocean claims amongst the five littoral states, the groundwork for the event having been carried out at an Oslo conference of senior officials of the five in October 2007. The governments of Sweden, Finland and Iceland, and Inuit representatives protested at their exclusion from the summit but were assured that this was an ad hoc meeting specifically focused on claims in the Ocean and not pulling up the rug of Arctic governance. This justification did appear to be supported by the statements that came out of the summit and the declaration that refers to the five's commitment to international law and the UN Convention on the Law of the Sea (UNCLOS) process to resolve disputes in the Ocean.

'Outsider' suspicions of an Arctic clique, though, recurred when a second 'A5 summit' was announced suddenly and at short notice by Canadian Foreign Minister Lawrence Cannon at Chelsea, Quebec, in 2010. The Chelsea summit did not add anything of substance to the Ilulissat Declaration, arousing suspicions that this was little more than a Canadian initiative to be at the centre of the new 'in crowd'. This was certainly the view of most outside of that crowd, with criticism from the excluded 'Arctic 3' added to by the ICC and the EU. The most stinging and significant criticism of A5 II, though, came from within the ranks of the new 'in crowd' at Chelsea, in the form of US Secretary of State Clinton (see Box 5.2).

Box 5.2 Hillary Clinton and Lawrence Cannon

Figure 5.2 Hillary Clinton and Lawrence Cannon

Cannon was made foreign minister by Stephen Harper in 2008 following two short-lived occupations of that post by successors of Peter MacKay. He was a surprise choice, having only entered parliament in 2006, but was a trusted right-hand man of Harper. Cannon had become the prime minister's 'Quebec Lieutenant' in 2005 in recognition of a prominent career in local politics, following the Canadian political custom of an Anglophone PM having a Francophone spokesman for Quebec. Cannon continued in this role alongside a transport portfolio in Harper's government until his elevation. His political descent was as rapid as his ascent when he was forced to leave government on losing his seat in the 2011 elections; however, he continues to play a role in Canadian diplomacy, having been appointed ambassador to France by Harper in 2012.

The presence of Hillary Clinton at Chelsea at first appeared to be a diplomatic triumph for Cannon, since the US tradition is to send a junior minister rather than the Secretary of State to Arctic summits. However, the appearance of one of the world's best-known politicians turned into a diplomatic own goal for him when she used the opportunity to berate the hosts for the exclusivity of the meeting and appealed that they 'should not create new divisions' (Clinton 2010). Clinton's words elevated the conference beyond what might normally be expected of an Arctic diplomatic event and earned her the praise of the Swedes, Icelanders, Finns and—most strikingly—the ICC.

Clinton's spectacular entrance into Arctic intergovernmental affairs probably has ensured that the Arctic Council's primacy will not be trumped by the A5. Cannon was forced to state as much in his closing remarks, notably delivered with Clinton already on the plane back to Washington rather than hanging around for the 'family photos'. It must have been tough for the Canadians to take being lectured to on inclusive diplomacy, multilateralism and indigenous rights by their southern neighbour. The Arctic Council was their initiative and one into which they had to drag the United States trailing their feet all the way. That the Council could get such a prominent endorsement from its least enthusiastic member must ultimately have seen it strengthened rather than weakened by the sudden ascent of the A5. The US stance is, though, not the volte-face it at first appears. Whilst being in a club of five rather than eight might appear to be in US national interest, they actually find themselves very much the outsider and underdog in this particular clique. The United States is not, of course, part of the continental shelf carve-up that chiefly defines the A5, and their key legal interest in the region is to open up full international access to the emerging Arctic sea routes, in line with the Arctic Ocean outsiders but not in line with the A5's most powerful players, Canada and Russia.

IR theory and Arctic intergovernmental cooperation

The theoretical discourse on the importance of IGOs represents, perhaps, the quintessential debate of International Relations (IR). IGOs have proliferated with globalization but, as with globalization itself, there are profound differences of opinion as to how significant this is in terms of understanding why international political events occur in the way that they do.

(Classical) Realism

To a large extent, Realist theory in International Relations was built on the core assumption that international organizations serve little purpose in the pursuit of peace and order in the world. The failure of the League of Nations to prevent the world slipping into the Second World War was considered by founding fathers of Realism, like Edward Carr and Hans Morgenthau, to demonstrate that organizations were not just irrelevant but also dangerous for international relations in giving a false sense of security. It was the employment of state force that was required to curb German, Italian and Japanese expansionism, not the open, multi-polar conference diplomacy of the Idealists. Intergovernmental organizations flourished after the Second World War, whilst Realism was in the ascendancy, but they were, predictably, less Idealist than those that made up the League of Nations system. The UN maintained the League's commitment to open diplomacy and the promotion of functional organizations to promote international commerce and relief, but it was infused with a heavy element of Realism in its peacekeeping functions. Balance of power logic was built into the Security Council, with five victorious great powers from the Second World War—the United States, USSR, UK, France and China—given special privileges in exchange for acting as world police. Hence, for Realists, the prolific growth of IGOs in the second half of the 20th century is not considered to be evidence of their increased significance since these organizations are not more than the sum of their parts.

This classical Realist scepticism of IGOs was, to some extent, revived in the 1990s when the end of the Cold War seemed to many to offer opportunities for a revitalization of the UN and other organizations. Notable among such sceptical voices was John Mearsheimer, who echoed similar sentiments to predecessors like Morgenthau in rebuffing the new Idealists: 'institutions have minimal influence on state behaviour and thus hold little promise for promoting stability in the post Cold War world' (Mearsheimer 1994: 7). Initial US antipathy to the AC and reflexive distrust of being accountable to UNCLOS arbitration could be viewed in classical Realist terms, as could the A5's apparent eschewing of the open diplomacy and institution building of the Arctic Council for a more closed, informal and exclusive forum.

(Neo)-Realism

The new breed of Realists who emerged alongside the onset of contemporary globalization from the 1970s gave more credence to the significance of IGOs in international relations, since their growth did appear to have made the political world seem more complex than that observed just by focusing on the state system. For writers like Gilpin (1981) and Waltz (1979), however, the significance of these new organizations did not lie in their capacity to erode state power and redefine state interests, but quite the opposite. Neo-Realists noted how many IGOs set up after the Second World War actually served as a means of projecting US power and influence and reinforcing their hegemony of international affairs. The key elements of the new UN system were sited in the United States and they were designed in such a way that US dominance was ensured. This was most explicit in the sphere of international political economy where the International Monetary

Fund (IMF) and World Bank were bankrolled by the United States but were also set up so that they could put 'their mouth where their money was' and use their wealth to control the new trading and monetary system. A similar phenomenon could be seen in the military domain with the emergence of the North Atlantic Treaty Organization (NATO) and other institutionalized regional alliances serving as vehicles for projecting US power. Far from moving us away from seeing IR as a state system governed by power, for Neo-Realists, the rise of IGOs served to reinforce this logic. It is possible to view the rise of Arctic intergovernmentalism through the lenses of Neo-Realist and English School[3] thinkers if it is considered that the world's two premier military powers have come to accept a balance of power, consolidating their influence in the region by playing constructive roles in vehicles like the AC which might limit their manoeuvres a little but help reinforce the status quo and keep other rising powers—like the EU or China—at a distance. Like the Concert of Europe in the 19th century or the EU or World Trade Organization (WTO) in the present age, perhaps Arctic institutions and regimes represent mutually convenient vehicles for states rather than evidence of creeping devolved global governance. Wegge, for example, opines that 'decades of interstate cooperation, absence of war and adherence to international law, possesses many of the features of Bull and Elster's understanding of a stable political order' (Wegge 2011: 167).

Liberalism

On the other side of the 'classic IR debate' from the Realists, Liberals see IGOs (and non-state actors in general) as challenging the notion of IR being determined by states and also welcome this change. As far back as the 18th century, Kant had identified a route to 'perpetual peace' through a triumvirate of republican democracy, trade and international organizations, and Idealists in the 1920s looked to put this philosophy into practice with the League of Nations system. The League's demise, however, prompted a similar demise in fortune for Liberalism in IR, with Realists assuming the ascendancy in the 1940s and 1950s.

From the 1960s, though, Liberalism in IR re-emerged in the guise of Pluralists, like Rosenau, Burton, Keohane and Nye, who viewed IGOs not only in Idealist terms, as a preferred path for IR, but also for the objective analytical reasoning that such organizations were demonstrably changing the nature of world politics. Keohane and Nye contended that the increased level of transactions between states had created conditions of 'complex interdependence' in the world which undermined the Realist model of international politics being determined by states pursuing their own interests irrespective of the interests of others. In addition, it was argued that 'transgovernmental relations' could now be observed in international politics due to increased cooperation between governments. This concept disposes not only with the notion of states representing no more than the interests of their governments, but also with the idea that governments themselves are coherent entities (Keohane and Nye 1971). Due to the increased prominence of IGOs in international relations it came to be contended that many governments were becoming disaggregated, as ministers or subsets of one government came to form alliances with parts of other governments which might be at odds with their own governmental partners. In the EU, for example, the regular contact and increasingly common interests that link ministers of the member states have often seen them act as transgovernmental blocs in Brussels, able to fashion coordinated policy beyond that which would be likely to emerge from conventional intergovernmental diplomacy conducted by foreign ministers or the heads of government. This process permits cross-border cooperation to grow through the phenomenon of *spill-over*, whereby integration snowballs from the force of example of seeing that international cooperation works to the benefit of all added to the logistical advantage of using established means of cooperation to replicate the process in other policy areas.

European integration is only loosely comparable to Arctic intergovernmental politics but there is little doubt that cross-border interactions amongst the A8 have gradually intensified and formalized since the intention to work together on 'common issues' was announced in the Ottawa Declaration. The A8 bar Russia are amongst the most democratic countries on Earth, linked by increasingly intertwined economic interests in the region and have seen their relations progressively routinized through the development of the Arctic Council. In addition, examples of transgovernmental relations can be seen in Arctic diplomacy if we consider how the Russian and particularly US governments have played much more constructive roles on climate change in the context of the AC than their presidents have on the global stage.

Marxism/Critical Theory

Marxist IR theorists are sceptical about the impact of IGOs since they see wider economic structures, rather than actors, as determining international events. Many Critical Theorists, a post-positivist offshoot of Marxism, do, however, share the Neo-Realist view that IGOs have significance in terms of serving the interest of powerful actors: 'one mechanism through which the universal norms of a world hegemony are expressed is the international organization' (Cox 1994: 137). In contrast to Neo-Realists, though, this perspective considers that the hegemony concerned is that of the world's economic elite, a transnational class of people, rather than particular states. This position came to acquire greater resonance in international economic affairs from the 1970s when the United States' pre-eminence started to diminish and yet economic organizations like the IMF and World Bank persisted and new ones like the WTO emerged. Vested interests were behind such organizations but they were the interests of big business across the world rather than direct projections of US foreign policy, it came to be argued. From such a standpoint it could be reasoned that Arctic governance is not so much characterized by intergovernmental politics, as by a carve-up of oil and gas revenues by a transnational elite comprising the A5 governments, Western multinational corporations and Russian state-owned companies.

Social Constructivism

Social Constructivists came to prominence by arguing that the importance of culture in international relations was ignored by the Realists, Liberals and Marxists. Sociologists have long reasoned that institutions moulded culture and the behaviour of individuals in a society through the process of *socialization*, and this came to influence IR thinking from the 1990s as globalization brought international institutions more into focus. Hence, IR thinkers like Ruggie came to reason that organizations develop their own culture which can come to socialize government representatives and redefine the interests of those administrations (Ruggie 1998). This view, then, reinforces the Liberal-Pluralist view that the very experience of regularized international diplomacy leads to compromises, horse trading and learning which makes IGOs more than just the sum of their parts, as Realists would have it. For Social Constructivists, then, there is support for the notion that IGOs can develop a 'life of their own' and become far more than flags of convenience for states.

Hence, the emerging Arctic polity has been described by Stokke and Honneland as a 'Functional and discursive regionality' (Stokke and Honneland 2007: 182), and by Dodds as a 'socio-material network' (Dodds 2012: 4). From this viewpoint, a culture has evolved from the discourse that has emerged from the role of indigenous groups and transnational communities of climate scientists, geologists, international lawyers and other experts and regularized coming together of diplomats and politicians from their capital cities below the Arctic Circle. This has empowered conventionally non-powerful actors like the Inuit and Arctic scientists, and also compromised the national interests of the conventionally powerful. Hence, we see the governments of the United States and Russia pulled into positions against their Realist instincts on climate change and health and in accepting binding regimes. Social Constructivism, though, is an approach that is not ideologically predisposed to see the succession of sovereignty with wider governance as good or bad in the same way as the Liberals or Realists. Sovereignty is a social construct rather than a material fact that is either lost or gained with an international political initiative. The AC Search and Rescue agreement and likely future binding agreements put obligations on the states of the region to share a little of their internal sovereignty by co-managing the seas but, at the same time, this may enhance their external sovereignty on the global stage by demonstrating inter-regional order and limiting the influence of external powers.

Conclusions

Intergovernmental cooperation has evolved significantly since Gorbachev's Murmansk address. The Arctic Council has emerged and metamorphosed into a formal IGO, and other forums and regimes have been initiated and grown. As discussed in Chapter 3, some lament the lack of clarity in this emergent polar governance system when set against the Antarctic Treaty but such a comparison is misleading since the Arctic is nothing like its antipodean counterpart and, in these circumstances, overlapping, predominantly soft law regimes could be viewed as both more realistic and appropriate. The Liberal Oran Young is firmly of this view:

> Such a complex, in contrast to a fully integrated governance system, is able to establish distinct regulatory provisions and decision making procedures that are well suited to the character of separate issues. It is also able to adapt on a piecemeal basis, adjusting the provisions of individual regimes or elements to handle changing circumstances relating to specific issues without raising questions about the viability of a larger and more encompassing governance system.
>
> (Young 2011a: 331)

Intergovernmental cooperation is becoming more piecemeal and 'messy' the world over as grand Liberal visions of governance through clearly defined organizations come to be compromised by the fact that not all the constituent parts share this vision. Regional IGOs like Mercosur (Mercado Común del Sur, or common market of the south) in South America, the Association of Southeast Asian Nations (ASEAN) or the EU today do not look as their original architects hoped, but they still exist and continue to evolve since some still share the vision and they at least represent vehicles of convenience for others. The UN will never be what Woodrow Wilson and the Idealists aspired to but it continues to advance new forms of global governance through a complex web of organizations and regimes involving all the sovereign states on Earth, albeit with differing levels of commitment. The EU has come to learn that 'one size fits all' approaches to international cooperation can work against the interests of both the most and least enthusiastic supporters of integration. The 'Europe of many circles' or 'Europe à la carte' approaches of permitting some states to opt out of ventures like a common foreign policy or single currency were originally a sop to the least enthusiastic members like Denmark and the UK and against the ethos of European integration, but ultimately it has become apparent that such developments can only emerge by permitting clubs within clubs. If such cooperative ventures still prove successful the spill-over logic can still be activated and the more cautious attracted on board. Hence, the EU integration process continues to advance cooperation in spite of a series of setbacks culminating in the euro currency crisis resulting from idealistic attempts to shoehorn the economies of some countries into a venture for which they were not ready. Even with such serious setbacks, few serious commentators can envisage the EU unravelling since the economies and interests of its constituent parts are so inter-related and a culture of working together to resolve common problems and have a united presence in the world has set in.

Arctic and European cooperation are apples and oranges but gradualist intergovernmental ventures tend to persist and grow. The world's oldest intergovernmental organizations—commissions for co-managing the Rhine and Danube established in the 19th century—are still going strong today. Co-managing a common resource like a river or ocean cuts costs and uncertainties and makes sense from nearly any IR perspective. The fact that Washington, Moscow, Beijing and Brussels along with non-governmental representatives of the region's indigenous peoples have all become supporters of the AC and its continued evolution provides evidence of that. The desire of the Nordic states for permanent secretariats for the AC and the BEAR, allied to the lack of strong objections from others and the recognition that it will actually save them time and effort, led to it happening. There is plenty of evidence around the world in general and the Arctic in particular to demonstrate that an instinctive reluctance to cooperate can be overcome, as long as everyone is on board and someone is willing to drive.

Notes

1 The Rules of Procedure, though, state that the number never exceed eight, the number of member states.
2 The members are: Oulu, Lapland and Kainuu from Finland; Finnmark, Nordland and Troms from Norway; Norrbotten and Vasterbotten from Sweden; and Murmansk, Arkhangelsk, Karelia, Komi and Nenets from Russia.
3 A UK-based (though not exclusively British) variant of Neo-Realism distinguished by a less positivist methodology, so permitting greater appreciation of normative influences on state behaviour.

6 Non-governmental cooperation

The rise and significance of transnational solidarity amongst the indigenous peoples and scientists of the Arctic

---

Box 6.1 ICC 2009 Declaration of Sovereignty

Figure 6.1 Logo of the Inuit Circumpolar Council

In 2009, motivated by the Ilulissat Summit and declaration the previous year which had 'neglected to include Inuit in a manner comparable to Arctic Council deliberations', the Inuit Circumpolar Council (formerly Conference) (ICC) released their own declaration stating a 'right to self-determination in the Arctic':

> For Inuit living within the states of Russia, Canada, the USA and Denmark/Greenland, issues of sovereignty and sovereign rights must be examined and assessed in the context of our long history of struggle to gain recognition and respect as an Arctic indigenous people having the right to exercise self-determination over our lives, territories, cultures and languages.

(ICC 2009)

Introduction

Contrary to appearance and the assumptions of most observers, this statement was not a declaration of Inuit national autonomy and, in fact, reveals a nuanced, contemporary attitude to sovereignty as a multi-faceted and evolving concept. As discussed in Chapter 4, in relation to indigenous peoples' land rights vis-à-vis their sovereign overlords, the declaration is not a call by the Inuit to replace that sovereignty with their own equivalent rule but an appeal to redefine the concept in a way that would, ultimately, serve the interests of both sides. Equally, in an international context, the Declaration is not a proclamation of independence so much as an appeal for the recognition of the reality of interdependence in the Arctic. It is more the pragmatic expression of diverse peoples thrown together by circumstances and common interests than a romanticized assertion of the cultural bonds that conventionally underpin national self-determination movements. It is not, as with most nationalist movements, an appeal by the Inuit to join the Westphalian system so much as an appeal by the Inuit to the Westphalian system to join them by evolving and adapting to a form more appropriate to a globalizing world. The sovereign states are asked not to step aside but to work alongside the Inuit as 'partners in the conduct of International Relations in the Arctic' (ICC 2009).

Whilst the Arctic states have been asserting their sovereign claims over the region, bringing more conventional—and some unconventional—intergovernmental politics to a region previously often marginalized from the Westphalian system, non-governmental politics has not been overridden. As already discussed in previous chapters, the new diplomacy of the Arctic states is influenced by the discourses of the region's indigenous peoples and also of the global environmental interaction promoted by the United Nations Environment Programme (UNEP) and global civil society actors. This chapter analyses the impact of transnational politics in the Arctic outside of, but nonetheless still related to, the more formal intergovernmental relations discussed in the previous chapter. The cross-border interactions and subsequent global political influence of two particular transnational communities are examined: the region's indigenous peoples; and scientists in the region who serve the international community rather than their own governments.

Transnational politics in international relations

Transnational politics refers to the realm of International Relations (IR) that exists outside of formal intergovernmental diplomacy. The term emerged from the 1970s through the contention of Liberal/Pluralist IR scholars that understanding government foreign policy-making, diplomatic exchanges and interaction in intergovernmental organizations (IGOs) was not enough to appreciate properly the politics of a globalizing world (Keohane and Nye 1971). The rise of cross-border interactions between non-governmental organizations (NGOs) outside of direct governmental control—including pressure groups, multinational corporations (MNCs), armed insurgencies and scientists serving the international community—for many necessitated seeing the political world as more than the conventional map image of nearly 200 competing sovereign units.

Pressure groups

Pressure groups with international political influence have grown hugely in recent decades from around 1,000 at the end of the Second World War to a figure of over 60,000 in the world today (UIA 2009), becoming key players in the emergence and evolution of international politics with regards to the environment, human rights and development. As well as holding governments of their home country to account, in the way that has come to be accepted as integral to modern democratic state governance, groups like Amnesty International, Greenpeace and Oxfam also influence the conduct of international relations by moulding the international political agenda through advancing issues outside of the obvious interest of governments and helping implement international law. Over 2,500 pressure groups have consultative status with the UN, which gives them the right to attend and contribute to important conferences. The 1992 UN Conference on the Environment & Development (UNCED) at Rio, the most significant international political event in the history of these two issue areas, was actually organized and managed by pressure groups on behalf of the UN. Groups like Amnesty have been pivotal in monitoring whether governments who have ratified international human rights conventions actually live up to their word after smiling for the cameras when signing up at the founding treaty.

The UN-pressure group relationship is a symbiotic one. The pressure groups benefit from the global exposure that the UN provides. The UN benefits from being able to draw upon the specialist and independent expertise the pressure groups can offer. Most high-profile pressure groups can boast a significant budget, usually drawn from individual donations, which gives them the capacity to hire high-quality professionals and make their presence felt in international political diplomacy without being tainted by association with parochial national interests. Amnesty, Greenpeace, Oxfam and many other groups have memberships in the millions and budgets in the tens of millions of US dollars, which, since they are focused on specific areas, buys them the expertise and means to rival even the wealthiest states. For Liberals, this represents the emergence of a global civil society which can check the excesses of governments in international politics in the same way that such groups have in Western liberal democracies, acting as what former UN Secretary-General Kofi Annan referred to as the 'conscience of the world'. Hence, in this view, pressure groups are central to the achievement of humane global governance in place of traditional practice in international relations dictated by state interests. As with the rise of all non-state actors and the phenomenon of globalization in general, however, not everyone is convinced that the political world has really changed or is set to do so. Neo-Realist Kenneth Waltz, for example, opined that 'States are not and never have been the only international actors. But then structures are defined not by all the actors that flourish within them but by the major ones' (Waltz 1979: 93–94).

For Realists, the notion of global civil society has little substance and IR continues fundamentally to be about inter-state politics dictated by power and national interests.

Whilst the rise of the notion of global civil society can principally be characterized as the export of Western NGOs to the developing world, in the Arctic the most significant transnational politics has been indigenous. The impact of the Inuit, Sami and others on domestic policy in Arctic states was discussed in Chapter 4 and such groups have also influenced circum-Arctic and even global policy. In popular IR parlance, representatives of around 150,000 widely scattered Inuit peoples have 'punched above their weight' in recent international diplomacy, although this metaphor is also wholly inappropriate given that this influence is purely normative and born of a culture that eschews coercive forms of politics.

The impact of Western pressure groups has been comparatively limited in the Arctic. The same sort of logistical limitations on sovereign assertions apply to pressure groups seeking to have a permanent role in the High North: the prohibitive costs of maintaining full-time premises and the influence of indigenous peoples. The WWF is the most prominent Western pressure group in the region, running a Global Arctic Programme co-administered by several offices in Arctic state capitals. The WWF has carved out this role by working closely with the Arctic Council (AC) and also acquiescing to an Inuit agenda. They are the one Western pressure group to have observer status in the AC and have worked with them extensively on many projects and publications, particularly in producing *Arctic Bulletin*. The WWF also notably does not support campaigns to ban oil exploration in the region and seal hunting, which are led by Greenpeace and supported by other pressure groups such as Friends of the Earth.

Hence, global civil society is limited in the Arctic in that there is no cosy alliance between the indigenous peoples and Western pressure groups against negative social and environmental encroachment. The Inuit have voiced their concerns over environmental change forcefully and eloquently but their position is akin to that of developing states in forging the sustainable development paradigm in the 1980s. The main concern of the Inuit elite is to secure their share in the responsible future exploitation of resources, rather than looking to prohibit it in the ways advocated by Greenpeace. Environmental pressure groups are often viewed as more imperialistic than the remote governments that administer them from afar. Campaigns dating back to the 1970s to restrict hunting in the name of biodiversity are particularly resented, resulting in a distinct lack of enthusiasm for contemporary activists protesting against oil exploration. Despite having some reservations about oil exploration in his country, Greenlandic diplomat Aqqaluk Lynge summarized the attitude of Inuit to Western environmental activists occupying rigs in Baffin Bay, stating, 'we are tired of being told by Greenpeace what to do and what not to do' (Carrell and Scott 2010).

Epistemic communities

A distinctive form of transnational politics comes from less formal associations of technical experts: epistemic communities. The study of epistemic communities was pioneered by Peter Haas in the 1980s who defined the phenomenon as a 'network of professionals with recognized expertise and competence in a particular domain and an authoritative claim to policy-relevant knowledge' (Haas 1992: 3). Haas demonstrated that the creation of the sea conservation regime the Mediterranean Action Plan (MAP) was a consequence of a grouping of like-minded ecologists and marine scientists who gained access to national administrations and the secretariat of the UNEP. In particular, North African governments overcame an initial hostility to a regime seemingly prioritizing pollution concerns over their development and smacking of European neo-colonialism. The epistemic community established the principles that came to be accepted by Mediterranean state governments in formulating the norms and rules of the MAP regime, namely that

'Mediterranean currents and wind patterns transmit pollutants across national borders and that these pollutants interfere with other uses of the sea (such as recreation, tourism, fishing and navigation) thereby necessitating coordinated national control policies' (Haas 1989: 381–82). Epistemic communities are most influential in environmental issues where the principles being established tend to be highly technical and scientific. In such cases, the epistemic community is empowered by being able to provide an understanding of areas that is better than governments and government-appointed scientists. Hence, the discovery of a hole in the Earth's ozone layer over Antarctica in 1985 and the consensus of international scientific opinion as to the causal role of chlorofluorocarbons (CFCs) in this process led to the formation of a robust and effective international regime curbing CFC use and production within two years. In such cases, a united, independent voice of recognized experts on an issue served to provide a clear understanding of a problem requiring a political response, overcoming any instinctive temptation for governments to avoid the costs involved by playing a free rider whilst others deal with it, or being 'in denial' about the problem. Hence, UNEP and other elements within the UN system have sought actively to develop such epistemic consensus through the creation of groupings such as the Intergovernmental Panel on Climate Change (IPCC). This interplay between UNEP and transnational scientists has come to be hugely influential in the development of Arctic governance and this is analysed later in the chapter.

The Inuit Circumpolar Council

The Inuit Circumpolar Council (formerly Conference) (ICC) was founded in 1977 to link together indigenous movements in the Arctic states. Its origins can be traced back to a mutual initiative of Greenlandic and Canadian Inuit activists four years earlier, when an Arctic People's Conference arose as an offshoot of the work of the International Working Group for Indigenous Affairs (IWGIA). Greenlandic Inuit rights activists Kleivan and Aaby from the IWGIA and academic Robert Petersen organized an event at the Danish parliament in Copenhagen. The IWGIA had been founded in 1968 and was based in Copenhagen, thus encouraging the body to develop a focus on the Greenlandic Inuit after having principally focused on Latin American tribes in its early years. The idea of such an international Inuit gathering had also been proposed earlier that year by the Federation of Natives North of 60 Canada and other native representatives, who then attended the Copenhagen conference along with Sami delegates from Norway,

Sweden and Finland (Dahl 2009: 37–38). Leading Inuit diplomat Aqqaluk Lynge is unequivocal on the significance of this landmark event and the important role played by endogenous as well as indigenous forces:

> The Arctic People's Conference was a turning point for us. We were first of all thinking of ourselves as 'Inuit' but Helge Kleivan urged us to include the Sami in our organizing efforts and he inspired us to consider ourselves part of a broader indigenous movement.
>
> (Dahl 2009: 37)

Box 6.2 Aqqaluk Lynge

Figure 6.2 Aqqaluk Lynge

The Greenlandic diplomat, activist and poet Aqqaluk Lynge, who has twice headed the ICC, has been, probably, the most prominent Inuit in international affairs over the past three decades.

In the 1970s and early 1980s, Lynge was a social worker, radio journalist and political activist, co-founding the leftist separatist Inuit Ataqatigiit party. He was first elected to the Greenland parliament (Landsting) in 1983, where he served in a number of roles including minister of social affairs in the government from 1984 to 1988. He left the Landsting in 1995 but was re-elected in 2002. Lynge is widely published in both political works and poetry and is also increasingly prominent on the global stage, representing his people in environmental negotiations and as a member of the UN Permanent Forum on Indigenous Issues (UNPFII).

Extract from 'For Honour and Glory'
They explored and explored
and travelled back
with maps of the country
and descriptions of the lifestyle
for honour and glory
for medals and degrees
for having explored a country
where people live and dwell.

(Lynge, in Hansen 2008: 16)

Two years after the Arctic People's Conference, the World Council of Indigenous Peoples was founded with a conference in Port Albemi, British Columbia, and pan-Inuit cooperation was further encouraged. At that event, the mayor of the recently empowered North Slope Borough in Alaska, Eben Hopson, gave notice that an international political gathering of the world's Eskimo would soon take place (ICC Canada 2012). Consequently, utilizing funding Hopson had secured from the philanthropist organization the Lilly Endowment, the first Inuit Circumpolar Conference took place in Barrow on 13–17 June, attended by 18 delegates each from Alaska, Canada and Greenland. Whilst this event was more specifically for the Inuit than the Arctic's indigenous peoples, Sami representatives also attended as observers and this was acknowledged in Hopson's opening speech:

> I am pleased that we have the Saami delegation with us today. The Saami have developed the kind of relationship with their governments that we seek with ours for the North American Inupiat community.
>
> (ICC Canada 2012)

The 54 delegates at Barrow passed 18 resolutions, the first of which unanimously agreed to make permanent their cooperation through the creation of an 'international organization of Inuit to study, discuss, represent, lobby and protect' them on the international stage (Resolution ICC-77-01). The other resolutions promoted the rights of indigenous peoples to access resources, information and health care, the right to roam across national boundaries, and home rule for Greenland. Also advocated was environmental protection but with the right to continue whaling, along with disarmament and an appeal to the USSR to permit the Siberian Inuit to participate in future conferences. The Soviet government had previously been approached on this via the US and Danish embassies but had never replied (Lynge 2012b). Unity amongst the Eskimo was the underlying theme of the conference, although observers noted that linguistic differences between the various groups was an obstacle in discussions (Wrenn 1978). This plus judicial differences between the three states delayed the launch of the ICC charter until the 2nd General Assembly at Nuuk, formally inaugurating the organization (Lynge 2012b). The name Inuit Circumpolar Conference was, initially, maintained for the new organization until it was changed to Council in 2006 to avoid the obvious confusion. The Russian Inuit were brought into the ICC family in 1989 after lobbying dating back to 1985 when Lynge visited Moscow. As an added consequence of this interaction with the changing Soviet Union, Mikhail Gorbachev's 1987 Murmansk speech was influenced by the ICCs Regional Conservation strategy launched two years earlier (Lynge 2012b).

The charter set out the aims of the ICC, which remain today:

- Strengthen unity among Inuit of the circumpolar region
- Promote Inuit rights and interests on an international level
- Ensure adequate Inuit participation in political, economic and social institutions
- Promote the greater self-sufficiency of the Inuit
- Ensure the endurance and the growth of Inuit culture and societies
- Promote long-term management and protection of Arctic and sub-Arctic wildlife, environment and biological productivity
- Promote wise management and use of non-renewable resources, taking into account other Inuit interests.

(Lynge 2012b)

In terms of organizational structure and process, an ICC General Assembly is held every four years, at which a Chair and eight-member Executive Council are elected to work at implementing new resolutions announced in a declaration. The ICC does not yet have a secretariat but an international office is run by the Chair and each member country also hosts an office headed by a president: ICC Canada, ICC Greenland, ICC Alaska and ICC Chukotka.

The declaration from the Kuujjuaq Assembly directed the ICC to make use of an array of international organizations to promote the rights and interests of the Inuit, although this was really a reaffirmation of a strategy they have long employed to good effect. In the UN, the ICC gained consultative status with the Economic and Social Council (ECOSOC) in 1983 and have subsequently played a prominent role at many UN conferences on environmental issues and human rights,

Table 6.1 Chronology of the ICC

Year	Venue	President/Chair	Key developments
1977	Barrow	Hopson (Alaska)	
1980	Nuuk	Rosing (Greenland)	ICC Charter inaugurated
1983	Iqaluit (Nunavut)		Event broadcast by Inuit Broadcasting Corporation
1986	Kotzebue (Alaska)	Simon (Canada)	Inuit Regional Conservation Strategy launched
1989	Sismiut (Greenland)		Chukotka Inuit join ICC
1992	Inuvik	MacLean (Alaska) replaced by Pungowiyi (Alaska) in 1993 due to ill health	Adopted principles and elements for a Comprehensive Arctic Policy
1995	Nome	Kuptana (Canada) 1997 Lynge (Greenland)	Call for greater international control of the nuclear industry
1998	Nuuk		Right to sustainable hunting
2002	Kuujjuaq (Nunavik)	Watt-Cloutier (Canada)	Call to work with IGOS and 'appropriate' NGOs
2006	Barrow (Utgiarvik declaration)	Cochrane (Alaska) 2009 Stotts (Alaska)	Support the adoption of UN Declaration on the Rights of Indigenous Peoples
2010	Nuuk		Promote the ICC Declaration of Sovereignty
2014	Nain, Labrador	2010 Lynge (Greenland)	

including assisting in the drafting of the Universal Declaration on the Rights of Indigenous Peoples. The Kuujjuaq Assembly also cited the importance of developing relations with the European Union (EU), the Organization of American States (OAS), the North American Free Trade Agreement (NAFTA), the International Whaling Commission (where they have had observer status since 1980), the Convention on Biological Diversity (CBD) and the World Intellectual Property

Organization (WIPO). The ICC also often works in conjunction with the Sami Council in global diplomacy as, for example, in the UN Forum for Indigenous Peoples, where they have for a number of years been jointly represented by a single delegate.

Relations with the EU have sometimes been fraught for the same reasons that strain Inuit-Western NGO relations, with EU legislation prohibiting the import of seal meat particularly resented. The Inuit, though, have managed to wield influence through the EU, even though Greenland has the notoriety of being the only country ever formally to step off the Euro-juggernaut. Cleverly, the ICC Greenland has employed the diplomacy of 'post-colonial embarrassment' to push the Danish government to negotiate an 'Inuit exemption' to the EU's seal products imports ban. Greenlandic diplomats present at negotiations in Brussels publicly raised the 'C Word' (colony) in the presence of other Europeans in order to push the Danish delegation into a position uncharacteristically out of step with their environmentalist instincts (Adler-Nissen 2012).

The AC, undoubtedly, is the IGO of most significance to the ICC and in the 2010 Nuuk Declaration they reasserted that they would 'continue to use the Arctic Council as a key arena to further the interests of the Inuit', and that the organ should be seen as 'the central forum for international cooperation in the Arctic' (ICC 2010). Their permanent participant status and voice within half of the member states gives them a useful political platform that they, predictably, cherish.

The Nuuk Declaration also reasserted the ICC's desire to work with rather than resist external economic forces in appealing that 'Inuit be educated and trained to participate significantly in the ownership, management and employment associated with those initiatives [development of non-renewable resources] and that royalties and other revenues derived from resource development be shared equitably with Inuit' (ICC 2010). The 2010 McKenzie valley natural gas pipeline proposal is an example of this being put into practice, being backed by the Aboriginal Pipeline Group, comprising representatives of the Inuvialuit, Gwich'in and Sahtu indigenous peoples, all securing a one-third stake in the project. Whilst, as discussed in Chapter 4, there are notable differences amongst them, overall the ICC wants the Inuit way of life respected but not necessarily preserved in pre-modern form. They are not averse to change if it is change for the better and are wary of being treated as an anthropological museum exhibit.

The foothold in land rights established by Arctic indigenous groups from the 1970s helped them gradually come to influence the growing global discourse on environmental issues from the early 1990s. Again, this influence emerged from working constructively with governmental and intergovernmental polities, particularly in the areas of persistent organic pollutants (POPs) and climate change. The ICC, though, was at this stage acknowledged as being at the forefront of sustainable development thinking, as evidenced by their receiving the UNEP Global 500 award in 1988 in recognition of the Inuit Regional Conservation Strategy (IRCS). The IRCS is rooted in the ethos of sustainably utilizing resources that came to define global environmental discourse from the mid-1980s, but includes assertions of the right to continue traditional hunting and fishing practices controversial to many global ecologists.

The discovery of high concentrations of POPs in Arctic peoples and the 'grasshopper effect' that takes them there, discussed in Chapter 3, was a notable output of the Northern Contaminants Program set up by the Canadian government with considerable input from indigenous groups. The programme was chaired by Indian and Northern Affairs Canada of Canada (ITC), ICC, Dene Nation and the Council of Yukon First Nations, alongside relevant arms of the federal government. The programme published the influential *Canadian Arctic Contaminants Assessment Report* in 1997. Fenge notes that this pitched many of these indigenous representatives in at the deep end of technical international diplomacy but served them well in later international POPs negotiations (Fenge 2003: 193).

As well as contributing local knowledge to the pot of global understanding, the ICC has often sought to put a human face on highly technical discussions. At the second meeting of the POPs negotiations in Nairobi, Sheila Watt-Cloutier, then president of ICC Canada, presented Klaus Topfer, executive director of UNEP and chair of the negotiations, with a carving of an Inuit mother and child which he placed on his desk for the delegates to consider during debate (Watt-Cloutier *et al.* 2005: 66–67).

Topfer himself is unequivocal on the influence of the ICC, not only on POPs but on global environmental politics in its entirety:

> Among the chief bell ringers was Sheila Watt-Cloutier. The Stockholm Convention on POPs is, in large part, testament to her tireless campaign on behalf of the Inuit people and the world to get POPs banned. It is a tribute to the power of civil society …
>
> The environment movement rides on the energy, input and commitment of civil society. Repeatedly, we have seen champions of environmental protection, such as Rachel Carson, Theo Colburn and Sheila Watt-Cloutier, compelling governments and the international community to look honestly at environmental problems caused by human activity and persuading them to take action to solve them.
> (Topfer's Foreword to IPEN 2007)

The combination of advancing local knowledge and shedding light on the human dimensions of environmental change has also been prominent in climate change diplomacy. Inuvialuit from Banks Island, Northwest Territories presented a video-recording showing the effects of climate change on their local environment and community at the 2000 Conference of the Parties (COP) of the UN Framework Convention on Climate Change (UNFCCC) in the Hague. ICC Greenland has, since 2005, been running the 'Sila-Inuk' project, which documents findings from Inuit hunters around the island on changes in the availability of resources, and 'Siku-Inuit-Hila' (sea ice-people-weather), which monitors sea ice changes (Lynge 2011: 194).

In 2005, the 'Many Strong Voices' programme on climate change was established linking the ICC with the Small Island Developing States (SIDS)—containing many low-lying tropical islands vulnerable to sea-level rises and, hence, fellow 'barometers' of global warming. The programme is not really non-governmental in that it is coordinated by UNEP/GRID-Arendal and the Centre for International Climate and Environmental Research funded by the Norwegian government, again highlighting the ICC's capacity for constructive engagement with the international community. Many Strong Voices has articulated its three central aims: an effective global agreement on climate change; respect for the use of traditional knowledge in understanding climate change; and financial and technical assistance from the world's most wealthy and culpable for the problem (MSV 2012). Building on this initiative and utilizing contacts established through the UN Forum for Indigenous Peoples, in 2009, the ICC organized the Indigenous Peoples Global Summit on Climate Change in Anchorage, which attracted 300 participants from over 70 countries around the world.

The ICC and other indigenous representatives are influential in the Arctic Council working groups and this, in turn, has been a big influence on global policy. Most notable has been the influence of the Inuit Regional Conservation Strategy on the Arctic Climate Impact Assessment (ACIA). Hence, we can see a symbiotic relationship between the ICC and Arctic Council both empowered by their mutual endorsements which serve to keep non-Arctic states and NGOs at a distance.

In perhaps the highest-profile international political initiative of the ICC to highlight the effects of global warming in 2005, they attracted global attention by serving a petition with the Inter-American Human Rights Commission against the US government, for their negligence in combating the problem. The legal case predictably came to nothing but the episode served its purpose in highlighting the human consequences of climate change through wide media coverage of the story. Following in this trend of attracting publicity for the cause, in 2007, the ICC even made a brief foray into UK politics when Lynge visited the country to add his opposition to plans to extend Stansted Airport on the grounds of averting climate change.

Other Arctic indigenous forums

The ICC is the most prominent voice of Arctic indigenous peoples on the world stage but other groups have also made a diplomatic impact, either independently or in conjunction with the Inuit. The Sami have links with the International Labour Organization and Working Group of Indigenous Peoples going back to the 1970s and have been the key catalyst for global policy on aboriginal rights. The UN's PFII was the brainchild of Swedish Sami Lars Anders Baer and its first chair was his Norwegian compatriot Ole Henrik Magga. Like the ICC, the Sami Council and Aleut International Association have consultative status with the UN via ECOSOC.

Arctic Indigenous Leaders Summits were initiated in 1991 just one week after the Arctic Environment Protection Strategy (AEPS) was given approval, bringing together several of the Arctic's indigenous peoples' groupings. The Sami Council and the predecessor of the Russian Association of Indigenous Peoples of the North, Siberia and Far East (RAIPON) were invited along by the ICC to a Summit in Hørsholm, near Copenhagen, establishing a process of meetings rotated every four to six years amongst the participating parties. As at the first ICC meeting, linguistic barriers affected debate and led to the agreement that English be accepted as the official working language. The second summit, at Tromsø, gave its support to the idea of an Arctic Council but, at the same time, insisted that indigenous groups be given a prominent role in the instrument. Since the inauguration of the AC and its conferring of a strong role for the indigenous groups, the Arctic Indigenous Leaders Summits have served as caucus meetings for those recognized 'permanent participants'. Hence, on joining the AC as permanent participants, the Aleut International Association began attending the summits in 1999 and the Arctic Athabaskan Council hosted the 2005 event in Montreal. Significantly, the 1999 and 2010 summits were hosted by RAIPON in Moscow, symbolizing a fuller involvement by Russian indigenous peoples in this process than the ICC, which has yet to be hosted by the Chukotka Inuit. As with the ICC, each summit is concluded with a declaration, most of which have been in line with ICC aims of ensuring the involvement of indigenous peoples in environmental policy and industrial development. The 2010 Moscow

Declaration included an appeal to UNEP to include the Arctic indigenous groups as a 'permanent presence' in its governing council (ALS 2010).

Indigenous voices have become more prominent the world over as a consequence of the evolution of the notion of aboriginal rights which has occurred as a knock-on effect of UN activities promoting decolonization through the Trusteeship Council and as part of the maturation of political discourse on development and environmental change. Arctic indigenous peoples, able to utilize platforms provided by inhabiting developed, largely democratic and diplomatically prominent states and their role in the Arctic Council, have found themselves better placed than most aboriginal people to take advantage of this.

International scientific cooperation in the Arctic

Box 6.3 Karl Weyprecht

Figure 6.3 Karl Weyprecht

Nineteenth-century Austro-German explorer Weyprecht can lay claim to being the father of international scientific cooperation in the Arctic region. Though born in German Hesse, Weyprecht served in the Austro-Hungarian navy as a young man, seeing action in the 1860s wars of Italian independence. In the early 1870s, his sense of maritime adventure led him to team up with Julius Von Payer to co-lead two Arctic expeditions funded by the Austro-Hungarian government, who were hoping to locate a North East Sea Passage.

The 1872–74 expedition saw the two men discover Franz Joseph Land (named after the Emperor) but the expedition ran into trouble when the ship became trapped in the ice. Weyprecht, Von Payer and surviving crewmen managed to travel from the stricken ship to Novaya Zemlya where they were eventually rescued by Russian sailors.

On his return, dissatisfied with the actual scientific value of his adventures, Weyprecht became a proponent of internationally co-sponsored and coordinated research, lamenting current expeditions as amounting to an: 'international steeplechase to the North Pole, a system opposed to true scientific discoveries' (Van Miegham and Landsberg 1958: 3). His ideas were presented at an 1873 meeting of the Association of German Naturalists and Physicians and prompted German Chancellor Bismarck to set up a commission to examine their feasibility. Private sponsorship and the support of other governments saw Weyprecht's vision become reality in 1879 with the launch of the International Polar Commission at an International Meteorological Congress in Rome. Weyprecht died the following year of tuberculosis before he could see the International Polar Commission launch the first International Polar Year of 1882–83.

(Kelley 2007: 1298)

The first International Polar Year (IPY), of 1882–83, saw 12 countries co-sponsor 14 simultaneous expeditions and 39 permanent observatories. In line with Weyprecht's proposals, information gathered from these initiatives was fed into a central commission and made available to the world. Fifty years later, a second IPY took place in the winter of 1932–33 involving 44 countries and extended the number of stations (IASC 2012). The third IPY, convened a quarter rather than half century on, in 1957–58, further progressed the number of countries involved (67), developed new international polar stations and took some huge scientific steps, such as confirming the theory of continental drift and discovering the Van Allen radiation belt around the Earth. The third IPY also, though, clearly demonstrated that polar collaboration in the north had slipped far behind that in the Antarctic. Special committees for Arctic and Antarctic research were proposed in order to coordinate polar activities given what was now the global rather than bi-regional scope of the re-styled International Geophysical Year. However, whilst the Special Committee for the Antarctic was duly established in 1958, paving the way for the 1959 Antarctic Treaty, the Arctic equivalent was stillborn owing to the geopolitical bifurcation of the region in the Cold War. Hence it was not until Gorbachev's Murmansk address of 1987 that truly circum-Arctic scientific cooperation could be reactivated.

Three years after Murmansk, the International Arctic Science Committee (IASC) came into being, some 32 years overdue, declaring its mission to 'encourage, facilitate and promote basic and applied interdisciplinary research in or concerned with the Arctic at a circumArctic or international level' (IASC 2012). The IASC is structured like a typical international organization, with an IASC Council comprising one representative each of the recognized national polar institutes from the 19 countries,[1] which meets once a year to steer overall activities, reaching agreements by consensus. Between Council meetings, held during Arctic Science Summit Week, an Executive Committee of five elected officials implements decisions and manages matters arising. A four-person secretariat, headed by an executive secretary, is hosted by the Norwegian government. Projects are organized through five working groups in the following areas: terrestrial, cryosphere, marine, atmosphere, and social and human. In addition to this, Biannual Science Symposia were inaugurated in 2009 at a meeting in Bergen.

The IASC is at the confluence of regional and global epistemic communities on POPs and climate change. Its sea impact studies on the Bering and Barents in the 1990s were a catalyst for regional cooperation that would culminate in the formation of the Arctic Council and on the work of the IPCC. They were the key architects of the Arctic Monitoring and Assessment Programme (AMAP) prior to the launch of the AC, and then, in conjunction with it, have managed the Arctic Climate Impact Assessment (ACIA), which has brought together over 300 researchers to produce 'trans-national scientific consistency on Arctic climate issues with a remarkably high level of agreement' (Stokke and Honneland 2007: 176). The IASC role in ACIA was also a crucial link between regional and global scientists since 'the global climate science regime strengthened the scientific legitimacy of the project while the regional scientific cooperation in IASC served as a bridge to the regional political cooperation in the Arctic Council' (Koivurova *et al.* 2009a: 84–85). The overlap between epistemic communities is also evident in terms of key personnel. This is most apparent in climate change where Swedish meteorologist Bert Bollin went from being a founding chair of the IPCC to become Vice-Chair of the IASC Executive Committee, and US scientist Robert Corell, who served on the IPCC before going on to lead the ACIA. In a graphic illustration of how such epistemic consensus can smooth out inter-governmental differences, the United States consistently has played a full part in this epistemic community in spite of its sometimes limited participation in the global political community on climate change, as evidenced by the siting of the ACIA secretariat in Fairbanks.

An intensification of international scientific activity in the Arctic is reflected in the fact that the start of the 2012 International Polar Year came just five years after the previous one. The desire to facilitate epistemic consensus has also been evident in the fostering of links between the IASC and other Arctic-based intellectual associations. In 2011, a formal partnership between the IASC, University of the Arctic and International Arctic Social Sciences Association (IASSA) was launched.

Conclusions

Whilst much of the world's political attention on the Arctic focuses on traditional intergovernmental geopolitics, there is little doubt that transnational politics is a key determinant of policy in the region. Transnational communities of indigenous peoples and international scientists do not figure on conventional geopolitical projections of the region but they have been key players in putting the Arctic 'on the map'. Whilst the Arctic state governments increasingly assert their sovereignty over the region, they do so in ways that take heed of and show respect for these transnational communities. Although the Arctic finds itself increasingly influenced by the outside world through externally driven environmental and social change, its inhabitants have also been empowered by these developments. The Inuit and Arctic scientists—the canaries in the mine—speak with an authority that commands the attention of the Arctic states and the wider world.

The Arctic's two transnational communities, as well as sharing certain characteristics, are also mutually reinforcing, as articulated by Lynge at the 2012 International Polar Year Conference:

I have worked with leading scientists and policy-makers providing them with an Inuit perspective on climate change, while at the same time learning from them ... This way of knowing is often referred to as 'traditional knowledge' and increasingly we use it in cooperation with 'western science'.

(Lynge 2012a)

Whilst indigenous people were included in the early International Polar Years, their role was principally to provide casual labour rather than informing the science (Shadian 2009: 44). The 2007–08 IPY, though, showed how their stock has risen with the recognition of the role played by 'polar residents, including polar indigenous people, in research, planning, observation, processing and implementation of the various datasets created through IPY projects' (ibid.: 50). Given this and the centrality of indigenous people in the Arctic Council working group assessments, Shadian concludes that Arctic policy is a synthesis of the 'interaction between indigenous agency and sustainable development policy' (ibid.: 51). Epitomizing this, the 2012 IPY launched a new initiative—the Indigenous Knowledge Exchange Programme, featuring panels chaired by indigenous delegates on a range of issues including food security, land use, wildlife and the showcasing of locally produced films.

The Arctic's recent arrival on the world stage is actually more about the latter extending the reach of its spotlight than the people of the north joining the show. Ontologically and epistemologically, those at the global front line of climate change are coming to influence the rest of the world. The need to understand global environmental change necessitates listening to and learning from those on the spot, most knowledgeable and most affected. It is not just this local knowledge itself, though, but also the way that it is generated that is empowering the Arctic transnational communities. Circum-Arctic scientists and indigenous peoples viewed the world through post-sovereign, postmodern lenses long before Liberal-Pluralist notions of transnational politics or Social Constructivism had entered the lexicon of International Relations. Weyprecht in the 1860s recognized that sovereign pride was an obstacle to a proper scientific understanding of the world when it came to polar exploration. Traditional Inuit culture is inherently anti-(IR)Realist and postmodern. Anthropological studies reveal that Inuit societies have long been built upon norms of cooperation, non-violent conflict resolution, social egalitarianism and the common ownership of land and resources (Stern 2010: 83–85). Growing up in remote, inhospitable climes reinforces the need for hospitable social relations. These attributes are, on a wider scale, gradually coming to be recognized as increasingly desirable and necessary for the whole world.

Note

1 The Arctic 8 plus: China, France, Germany, Italy, Japan, Netherlands, Poland, South Korea, Spain, Switzerland and the UK.

7 Conclusions

Coming in from the cold

The Arctic is coming in from the cold, both literally and metaphorically, with climate change bringing both great change and great interest to a place previously very much on the margins of international relations. Whilst the region experiences global warming at twice the rate of the rest of the world to the south, it is experiencing the social and political implications of this at an even greater rate. For the High North, globalization is coming late but quickly. Rapid environmental change is radically transforming the landscape and the lifestyles of its human and non-human inhabitants. It is also bringing much more of the world below the Arctic Circle to the High North in a rapid economic, social and political encroachment into this once largely ignored wilderness. Although the Arctic lands have long been carved up between the sovereign powers, many of the people who inhabit them have, nevertheless, been left largely to their own devices. The prospect of easier access to resources thought previously to be inaccessible has reawakened interest in the region from the sovereign powers and from other powers outside of the region.

However, the 'new Cold War' scenarios of the Arctic coming to be despoiled in a new oil rush, widely predicted at the time of the Russian robotic North Pole landing in 2007, seem, just five years later, to be absurd and hysterical. The prospect of new oil and gas supplies becoming available allied to classic Western assumptions about Russian foreign policy prompted geopolitics traditionalists to assume the worst and dust down their Cold War lexicons. Such pessimism, whilst supported by much historical precedent, demonstrably is misplaced in observing the emerging international politics of the Arctic, characterized by intergovernmental cooperation and an inclusive discourse in which local and expert non-governmental organization (NGO) voices are prominent. Indeed, a peaceful Arctic should not come as a surprise given, as Byers observes, that we are talking about:

a vast, sparsely populated region with only a handful of nation-states; only a few, relatively minor boundary disputes; and a pre-existing framework of universally accepted international rules, centrally including the law of the sea. If humanity cannot cooperate in the Arctic, it cannot cooperate anywhere.

(Byers 2010: 128)

Whilst many see this as a clear vindication of Liberal International Relations (IR) theory, it is still possible to interpret this cooperative, legalistic emerging Arctic politics in Realist terms, in its more subtle 'English School' or 'Structural Realism' forms. Intergovernmental cooperation between five or eight states for their mutual gain, through the Arctic Council or less formally elsewhere, could be viewed as the politics of national interest carried out by a 'society of states'. Closer inspection of the international politics of the Arctic, though, reveals a picture much more complex than a great power 'Concert of the Arctic'. The Arctic Council is intergovernmental, with no supranational authority comparable to elements of the European Union or World Trade Organization, but it is strengthening and developing its own political personality, pulling recalcitrant governments into a consensual line. Its decisions require unanimity but its outputs are more than a lowest common denominator, producing contributions to international environmental governance beyond what might otherwise be anticipated for a forum including the United States and Russia. In addition, this consensus is not just arrived at between the eight, in the manner of classic intergovernmental horse-trading, since around the table are also representatives of the region's indigenous peoples who, whilst not taking the decisions, are clearly influencing them and also helping to set the agenda.

International politics in the Arctic is not, then, purely intergovernmental since the governments concerned are mindful of the opinions of indigenous peoples and transnational scientists who, whilst not conventionally powerful, carry normative and intellectual weight on the global as well as the regional stage. A symbiotic relationship between the region's indigenous NGOs and governments has emerged which underpins the new international politics. The sovereign claims of governments are reinforced by the Inuit and others inhabiting the frozen reaches simply being there, and having them 'on board' politically enhances their legitimacy as responsible stewards of the changing landscape to an increasingly interested world. For the indigenous peoples, this influence vis-à-vis their sovereign overlords and the Arctic Council, allied to their growing global presence as a United Nations discourse on aboriginal rights evolves, gives them the platform they need to advance their interests. In this way, we see international political pluralism and also social constructivism at work. Sovereignty and globalization are being reinterpreted as the multi-faceted and subjective concepts that they clearly are. Government sovereignty in the Arctic needs to be exercised in a measured, cooperative and inclusive manner if it is to succeed and this need not preclude the simultaneous assertion of indigenous 'sovereignty', as expressed in the Inuit Declaration of 2009. Both can assert their interests in the region in a mutually beneficial way which serves also to limit unwanted intrusions from the wider world calling for global rather than regional governance. Globalization threatens indigenous life in the Arctic, through environmental and social change, but also brings great opportunities and can be harnessed to highlight their cause. Hence, whilst a Marxist analysis of globalization as a relentlessly exploitative force seems at first vindicated by the plight of the Arctic's 'colonized', the agency of these people in making their voices heard in order to curb the excesses and enjoy the benefits of the phenomenon limits its applicability.

The Arctic becoming globalized, also, is a two-way phenomenon and not merely a case of the world and its practices, good and bad, heading north. The emerging international politics of the Arctic, rather than mimicking the worst of the past in the rest of the world, can more readily be viewed as a testing ground for a new kind of governance, increasingly needed the world over.

> [The] Arctic has emerged as a site of innovative political experi-
> mentation where national governments, indigenous peoples, and
> nongovernmental actors are exhibiting exceptional creativity in
> adapting to a complex and dynamic set of cultural and geophysical
> environments. Consequently, new and progressive practises and
> institutions are materializing to guide the region through future
> challenges. The world could do well to learn from the Arctic
> example.
>
> (Steinberg *et al.* 2012)

We are saddened to see the Arctic becoming more like us—and with good reason—but the story is not all bad for the people who inhabit it and, for us, being closer to them can only be beneficial.

Bibliography

ACPB (2009) *Meeting of the Parties to the 1973 Agreement on the Conservation of Polar Bears*, Tromsø, Norway, 17–19 March.

Adler-Nissen, R. (2012) 'Diplomacy as Impression Management: Strategic Face-Work and Post-Colonial Embarrassment', CIPSS Working Paper Series, 38, Center for International Peace and Security Studies Montreal: McGill University.

AEPS (1991) *First Ministerial Conference on the Protection of the Arctic Environment, Rovaniemi Declaration: Declaration on the Protection of the Arctic Environment*, 14 June.

——(2001) 'Arctic Environmental Protection Strategy', *International Legal Materials* 30: 1624.

ALS (2010) *Moscow Declaration*, V Arctic Indigenous Leaders Summit, Industrial Development of the Arctic Under Climate Change—New Challenges for Indigenous Peoples, 14–15 April.

Althingi (2011) 'Parliamentary Resolution on Iceland's Arctic Policy', 139th legislative session, 28 March, approved.

Anaya, J. (2011) *Human Rights Council Report of the Special Rapporteur on the Situation of Human Rights and Fundamental Freedoms of Indigenous Peoples. The Situation of the Sami People in the Sapmi Region of Norway, Sweden and Finland*, 12 January, HRC, United Nations.

Anderson, A. (2009) *After the Ice: Life, Death and Geopolitics in the Arctic*, Smithsonian: New York.

Arctic Biodiversity (2010) *Arctic Biodiversity Trends 2010*, www.arcticbiodiversity. is/ index.php/en/the-report.

Arctic Council (2012) 'Terms of Reference of the Arctic Council Secretariat', DMM02, 15 May, Stockholm.

Armstrong, S., Marcot, B. and Douglas, D. (2007) 'Forecasting the Range-wide Status of Polar Bears at Selected Times in the 21st Century', Administrative Report, Reston, VA: US Geological Survey.

Åtland, K. (2008) 'Mikhail Gorbachev, the Murmansk Initiative, and the Desecuritization of Interstate Relations in the Arctic', *Cooperation and Conflict* 43(3): 289–311.

Åtland, K. and Ven Bruusgaard, K. (2009) 'When Security Speech Acts Misfire: Russia and the Elektron Incident', *Security Dialogue* 40(3): 333–54.

Baev, P. (2010) 'Russian Policy in the Arctic. A Reality Check', in D. Trenin and P. Baev, *The Arctic. A View from Moscow*, Washington: Carnegie Endowment for International Peace.

Baker, P. (2004) 'Putin Moves to Centralize Authority; Plan Would Restrict Elections in Russia', *Washington Post*, 14 September: A01.

Balzer, M. and Vimokurova, U. (1996) 'Nationalism, Interethnic Relations and Federalism: The Case of the Sakha Republic (Yakutia)', *Europe-Asia Studies* 48: 101–20.

Bartels, D. and Bartels, A.L. (2006) 'Indigenous Peoples of the Russian North and Cold War Ideology', *Anthropologica* 48(2): 265–80.

BEAR (2012) *Barents Euro-Arctic Region*, www.beac.st/in_English/Barents_Euro-Arctic_Council.iw3 (accessed 18 September 2012).

Bindoff, S. (1982) *Tudor England*, Harmondsworth, UK: Penguin.

Blonden, M. (2012) 'Geopolitics and the Northern Sea Route', *International Affairs* 88(1): 115–29.

Borgerson, S. (2008) 'Arctic Meltdown', *Foreign Affairs* 87(2): 63–77.

Broderstad, E. and Dahl, J. (2004) 'Political Systems', in *Arctic Human Development Report*, Akureyri, Iceland: Stefansson Arctic Institute, 121–38.

Byers, M. (2010) *Who Owns the Arctic? Understanding Sovereignty Disputes in the North*, Vancouver: Douglas & McIntyre.

——(2011) 'Cooling Things Down: The Legalization of Arctic Security', paper presented at conference, Carnegie Council's Programme on US Global Engagement. A Two Year Retrospective, www.carnegiecouncil.org/resources/articles_papers_reports/0102.html (accessed 19 November 2011).

Canadian Government (2009) *Comprehensive Northern Strategy: Our North, Our Heritage, Our Future*, Ottawa.

Carrell, S. and Scott, K. (2010) 'Greenpeace Activists Arrested After Abandoning Occupation of Arctic Oil Rig', *The Guardian*, 2 September.

Cathcart, B. (2007) 'The Greening of Greenland', *New Statesman*, 13 September.

Caulfield, R. (2004) 'Resource Governance', in *Arctic Human Development Report*, Akureyri, Iceland: Stefansson Arctic Institute, 121–38.

CCGSS (2011) *Rethinking the Top of the World. Arctic Security Public Opinion Survey Final Report*, Toronto: Canada Centre for Global Security Studies, Munk University of Toronto.

China (2010) *China's View on Arctic Cooperation*, www.fmprc.gov.cn/eng/wjb/zzjg/tyfls/tfsxw/t812046.htm (accessed 23 August 2012).

Christensen, S. (2009) 'Are the Northern Sea Routes Really the Shortest?' *DIIS Brief*, Danish Institute for International Studies: Copenhagen.

Chryssochoou, D. (2007) 'Democracy and the European Polity', in M. Cini (ed.) *European Union Politics*, second edn, Oxford: Oxford University Press.

CIA (2012) *Jan Mayen*, World Factbook, www.cia.gov/library/publications/the-world-factbook/geos/jn.html (accessed 12 October 2012).

Clinton, H. (2010) Ilulissat Summit, reported in 'US, Canada at Odds Over Arctic Forum', Associated Press, 29 March.

Cohen, A. (2008) 'Russia's Race for the Arctic', *Heartland* 2: 28–36.

Cox, M. (1994) 'Gramsci, Hegemony and International Relations', in S. Gill (ed.) *Gramsci, Historical Materialism and International Relations*, Cambridge: Cambridge University Press, 124–43.

Dahl, J. (2009) *IWGIA. A History*, Copenhagen: International Work Group for Indigenous Affairs.

Denmark Government (2008) *Arktis i en brydningstid Forslag til strategi for aktiviteter i det arktiske område*.

Diamond, J. (2005) *Collapse. How Societies Choose to Fail or Succeed*, New York: Viking.

Ditmer, J., Moisio, S., Ingram, A. and Dodds, K. (2011) 'Have You Heard the One About the Disappearing Ice? Recasting Arctic Geopolitics', *Political Geography* 30(4): 202–14.

Dodds, K. (2010) 'Flag Planting and Finger Pointing: The Law of the Sea, the Arctic and the Political Geographies of the Outer Continental Shelf', *Political Geography* 29: 63–73.

——(2012) 'Anticipating the Arctic and the Arctic Council: Pre-emption, Precaution and Preparedness', *Polar Record*: 1–11.

Drevnick, P.E., Muir, D.C.G., Lamborg, C.H., Hogan, M.J., Canfield, D.E., Boyle, J.F. and Rose, N.L. (2010) 'Increased Accumulation of Sulfur in Lake Sediments of the High Arctic', *Environmental Science and Technology* 44 (22): 8415–21.

Duffy, R. (1988) *The Road to Nunavut: The Progress of the Eastern Arctic Inuit since the Second World War*, Montreal: McGill-Queen's University Press.

Eccleston, P. (2008) 'Campaign to Stop Greenland Seabird Slaughter', *Guardian* 1 May.

EEC (1985) 'Treaty Amending, with Regard to Greenland, the Treaties Establishing the European Communities', *Official Journal of the European Communities* 1(2).

Emmerson, C. (2010) *The Future History of the Arctic*, London: The Bodley Head.

Encyclopaedia Britannica (2005) 'Arctic', *Macropedia* 14: 1–37.

EU (2008) *The European Union and the Arctic Region*, Communication from the European Commission to the Parliament and Council, COM 763, Brussels, 20 November.

FAO (2009) *State of the World's Forests 2009*, Rome: Food and Agriculture Organization.

FCO (2012) *Global Issues. The Arctic*, UK Foreign and Commonwealth Office, www.fco.gov.uk/en/global-issues/polar-regions/uk-engagement-arctic/ (accessed 8 May 2012).

Fenge, T. (2003) 'POPs and Inuit: Influencing the Global Agenda', in D.L. Downie and T. Fenge (eds) *Northern Lights Against POPs: Combating Toxic Threats in the Arctic*, Quebec: McGill-Queens University Press.

Fikkan, A., Osherenko, G. and Arikainen, A. (1993) 'Polar Bears. The Importance of Simplicity', in O. Young and G. Osherenko (eds) *Polar Politics. Creating International Environmental Regimes*, Ithaca, NY: Cornell University Press, 96–151.

Finland Government (2010) *Finland's Strategy for the Arctic Region*, Helsinki: Prime Minister's Office Publications 8/2010.

Friborg, J. and Melbye, M. (2008) 'Cancer Patterns in Inuit Populations', *The Lancet Oncology* 9(9): 892–900.

Galeotti, M. (2008) 'Cold Calling. Competition Heats Up for Arctic Resources', *Jane's Intelligence Review* (October): 8–15.

Gao, Y., Drange, H., Johannssen, O. and Petterssen, L. (2009) 'Sources and Pathways of Sr in the North Atlantic-Arctic Region: Present Day and Global Warming', *Journal of Environmental Radioactivity* 100: 375–95.

Giddens, A. (1990) *The Consequences of Modernity*, Stanford: Stanford University Press.

Gilpin, R. (1981) *War and Change in World Politics*, Cambridge: Cambridge University Press.

Glasby, G. and Voytekhovsky, Y. (2010) 'Arctic Russia: Minerals and Resources', *Geoscientist* 8.

Gorbachev, M. (1987) Speech at the 'Ceremonial Meeting on the Occasion of the Presentation of the Order of Lenin and the Gold Star to the City of Murmansk', Murmansk, 1 October.

Governments of Denmark, Faeroes and Greenland (2011) *Strategy for the Arctic 2011–2020*, Copenhagen.

Grant, S. (2010) *Polar Imperative: A History of Arctic Sovereignty in North America*, Vancouver: Douglas & McIntyre, 418.

Statistics Greenland (2011) *Greenland in Figures*.

Grygier, P. (1994) *A Long Way from Home: The Tuberculosis Epidemic Among the Inuit*, Quebec: McGill-Queens University Press.

Haas, P. (1989) 'Do Regimes Matter? Epistemic Communities and Mediterranean Pollution', *International Organization* 43(3): 377–403.

——(1990) 'Obtaining International Environmental Protection Through Epistemic Consensus', *Millennium* 19(3).

——(1992) 'Epistemic Communities and International Policy Coordination', *International Organization* 46(1): 1–35.

Hagendoorn, L., Poppe, E. and Minescu, A. (2008) 'Support for Separatism in Ethnic Republics of the Russian Federation', *Europe-Asia Studies* 60(3) (May): 353–73.

Hansen, K. (2008) *Nuussarmiut-Hunting Families on the Big Headland*, Copenhagen: Commission for Scientific Research in Greenland.

Hardin, G. (1968) 'The Tragedy of the Commons', *Science* 162: 1243–48.

Hasanda, W. (2009) 'Towards Model Arctic Wide Environmental Cooperation Combating Climate Change', *Yearbook of International Environmental Law* 20(1): 122–57.

Hechter, M. (2000) *Containing Nationalism*, Oxford: Oxford University Press.

Humphreys, D. (2006) *Logjam. Deforestation and the Crisis of Global Governance*, London: Earthscan.

IASC (2012) *IASC Handbook*.

ICC (2009) *Declaration of Sovereignty*, Inuit Circumpolar Council, 28 April.

——(2010) *Nuuk Declaration*, Inuit Circumpolar Council, 2 July, www.inuit. org/index.php?id=409 (accessed 4 August 2012).

ICC Canada (2012) *ICC's Beginning*, Inuit Circumpolar Council Canada, inuitcircumpolar.com/section.php?ID=15&Lang=En&Nav=Section (accessed 12 June 2012).

ILO (2008) *Convention 169 Sami Ilulissat Declaration*, Governments of Denmark, Norway, Russia, United States and Canada, 28 May, arctic-council.org/ filearchive/Ilulissat-declaration.pdf (accessed 12 May 2011).

IPCC (2000) *Land-use, Land-use Change and Forestry. Special Report*, Cambridge: Cambridge University Press.

——(2007) *Fourth Assessment Report Climate Change*, Intergovernmental Panel on Climate Change.

IPEN (2007) 'Klaus Topfer UNEP Executive Director, Foreword', in *Citizen's Guide to the Stockholm Convention Civil Society Works to Eliminate Persistent Organic Pollutants (POPs)*, Berkeley: International POPS Elimination Network.

Jacobson, L. (2010) 'China Prepares for an Ice-Free Arctic', Stockholm: SIPRI.

Jeffers, J. (2010) 'Climate Change and the Arctic: Adapting to Changes in Fisheries Stocks and Governance Regimes', *Ecology Law Quarterly* 37: 917–78.

Jensen, L. and Skedsmo, P. (2010) 'Approaching the North: Norwegian and Russian Foreign Policy Discourses on the European Arctic', *Polar Research* 29: 439–50.

Johnsen, K., Alfthan, B., Hislop, L. and Skaalvik, J. (eds) (2010) *Protecting Arctic Biodiversity. Limitations and Strengths of Environmental Agreements*, Arendal, Norway: UNEP/GRID.

Kelley, J. (2007) 'The International Polar Year: A Legacy of Sydney Chapman', *The Leading Edge* 26(10) (October): 1298–300.

Kempton, D. and Clark, T. (2002) *Unity or Separatism: Center-Periphery Relations in the Former Soviet Union*, Westport, USA: Praeger.

Keohane, R. and Nye, J. (1971) *Transnational Relations and World Politics. An Introduction*, Cambridge, MA: Harvard University Press.

Keskitalo, C. (2007) 'International Region-building: Development of the Arctic as an International Region', *Cooperation and Conflict* 42(2): 187–205.

Koivurova, T. (2008) 'Alternatives for an Arctic Treaty. Evaluation and a New Proposal', *Review of European Community and International Environmental Law* 17(1): 14–26.

——(2009) 'Limits and Possibilities of the Arctic Council in a Rapidly Changing Scene of Arctic Governance', *Polar Record* 46: 146–56.

——(2010) 'Sovereign States and Self-Determining Peoples: Carving Out a Place for Transnational Indigenous Peoples in a World of Sovereign States', *International Community Law Review* 12: 192–212.

Koivurova, T., Carina, E., Keskitalo, H. and Bankes, N. (eds) (2009a) *Climate Governance in the Arctic*, New York: Springer.

Koivurova, T., Keskitalo, E. and Bankes, N. (2009b) *Climate Governance in the Arctic*, Hannover: Springer.

Kraska, J. (2011) *Arctic Security in an Age of Climate Change*, Cambridge: Cambridge University Press.

Krasner, S. (1983) *International Regimes*, Ithaca and London: Cornell.

Krummel, E. (2009) 'The Circumpolar Inuit Health Summit: A Summary', *International Journal of Circumpolar Health* 68(5): 509–18.

Kucera, J. (2009) 'Oil on Ice', *Atlantic Magazine* (November), www.theatlantic. com/magazine/toc/2009/11 (accessed 17 July 2011).

Law, A.K. and Stohl, A. (2007) 'Arctic Air Pollution: Origins and Impacts', *Science* 315: 1537–940.

Loukacheva, N. (2007) *The Arctic Promise: Legal and Political Autonomy of Greenland and Nunavut*, Toronto: University of Toronto Press.

Lynge, A. (2011) *Encyclopedia of Climate Change*, 2nd edn, Oxford: Oxford University Press.

——(2012a) *Keynote Speech International Polar Year Conference*, Montreal, 24 April, inuit.org/en/news/april-24-2012-aqqaluks-keynote-speech-at-ipy-2012. html (accessed 4 July 2012).

——(2012b) Personal communication, 9 September.

McGovern, T. (1980) 'Cows, Harp Seals, and Churchbells: Adaptation and Extinction in Norse Greenland', *Human Ecology* 8(3): 245–75.

Marshall, M. (2011) '2011 Arctic Hole was Biggest Ever', *New Scientist* 212 (2835): 9.

Mearsheimer, J. (1994) 'The False Promise of International Institutions', *International Security* 19(3).

Mikkelsen, A. and Langhelle, O. (2008) *Arctic Oil and Gas. Sustainability at Risk?* New York: Taylor & Francis.

Minde, H. (2005) 'Assimilation of the Sami-Implementation and Consequences', *Galdu Cala Journal of Indigenous People's Rights* 3 (Kautokeino, Norway: Resource Centre for the Rights of Indigenous Peoples).

Moller, H. (2010) 'Tuberculosis and Colonialism. Current Tales About Tuberculosis and Colonialism in Nunavut', *Journal de la Sante Autochton Native Aboriginal Health Organization*: 38–48.

Möller, S. (2008) *Press Release after Ilulissat Declaration*, 28 May, Ilulissat, Greenland.

MSV (2012) *Many Strong Voices*, www.manystrongvoices.org (accessed 5 August 2012).

Murphy, C. (1947) 'The Polar Concept. It is Revolutionizing American Strategy', *Life* (20 January): 61–62.

Nord, D. (2006) 'Canada as a Northern Nation: Finding a Role for the Arctic Council', in James, Michaud, O'Reilly (eds) *Handbook of Canadian Foreign Policy*, Oxford: Lexington, 289–315.

North Sky Consulting Group (2009) *Qanukkanniq (What Next)? The GN Report Card.*

Norway Government (2006) *High North Strategy*, Oslo.

Nunavut (2008) *Nunavut's Health System. A Report Delivered as Part of Inuit Obligations Under Article 32 of the Nunavut Land Claims Agreement 1993*, Iquailut: Nunavut Tunngavik.

Parker, R.D. and Madjd-Sadjadi, Z. (2010) 'Arctic: Sovereignty, Navigation and Land Claim Disputes', *Polar Record* 46(239): 336–48.

Pearce, F. (2005) 'Climate Warning as Siberia Melts', *New Scientist* (11 August).

Petersen, R. (1995) 'Colonialism as Seen from a Former Colonized Area', *Arctic Anthropology* 32(2): 118–26.

Pika, A. and Prokhorov, B. (1988) 'The Big Problems of the Small Peoples', *Kommunist* 16: 76–83.

Potts, T. and Schofield, C. (2008) 'Current Legal Developments: The Arctic', *The International Journal of Marine and Coastal Law* 23: 151–76.

RAIPON/IWGIA (2011) *Parallel Information Concerning the Situation of the Economic, Social and Cultural Rights of Indigenous Small-numbered Peoples of the North*, 46th Session of the Committee on Economic, Social and Cultural Rights, United Nations, 2–20 May.

Rethmann, P. (2004) 'A Dream of Democracy in the Russian Far East', in M. Blaer, H. Fiet and G. McRae, *In the Way of Development: Indigenous Peoples, Life Projects and Globalization*, London and New York: Zed Books.

Roo, C., Cavalieri, S., Wasserman, M., Knoblauch, D., Baush, C. and Best, A. (2008) *Background Paper: Environmental Governance in the Marine Arctic*, Arctic Transform EU.

Rothwell, D. (1996) *The Polar Regions and the Development of International Law*, Cambridge: Cambridge University Press.

Ruggie, J. (1998) *Constructing the World Polity. Essays on International Institutionalization*, London and New York: Routledge.

Russian Government (2009) *Fundamentals of Russian State Policy in the Arctic up to 2020 and Beyond*, Moscow.

Sakharov, A. (1990) *Memoirs*, New York: Alfred A. Knopf.

Sandberg, A. (2008) 'Collective Rights in a Modernizing North—On Institutionalizing Sami and Local Rights to Land and Water in Northern Norway', *International Journal of the Commons* 2(2): 268–87.

Sands, P. (2003) *Principles of International Environmental Law*, 2nd edn, Cambridge: Cambridge University Press.

Seale, P., Shellenberger, S. and Spence, J. (2006) 'Alcohol Problems in Alaska Natives: Lessons from the Inuit', *American Indian and Alaska Native Mental Health Research: The Journal of the National Center* 13(1).

Shadian, J. (2009) 'Revisiting Politics and Science in the Poles: IPY and the Governance of Science in post-Westphalia', in J. Shadian and M. Tennberg, *Legacies and Changes in Polar Sciences. Historical, Legal and Political Reflections on the International Polar Year*, Farnham, UK and Burlington, USA: Ashgate.

——(2010) 'From State to Polities: Reconceptualizing Sovereignty Through Inuit Governance', *European Journal of International Relations* 16(3): 485–510.

Sharma, S. (2010) 'Assessing Diet and Lifestyle in the Canadian Arctic Inuit and Inuvialuit to Inform a Nutrition and Physical Activity Intervention Programme', *Journal of Human Nutrition and Dietetics* 23, special supplement (7 September): 5–17.

Silviken, A. (2009) 'Prevalence of Suicidal Behaviour Among Indigenous Sami in Northern Norway', *International Journal of Circumpolar Health* 68(3): 204–11.

Skre, O., Baxter, R., Crawford, R.M., Callaghan, T.V. and Federokov, A. (2002) 'How Will the Tundra-Taiga Interface Respond to Climate Change?' *Ambio*, Special Report 12: 37–46.

Smith, A. (1995) *Nations and Nationalism in a Global Era*, Cambridge: Polity.

Smith, J., Brandon, M. and Kurtz, M. (2009) *Arctic Approach*, Milton Keynes: Open University Press.

Smol, J. and Douglas, M. (2007) 'From Controversy to Consensus: Making the Case for Recent Climate Change in the Arctic Using Lake Sediments', *Frontiers in Ecology and the Environment* 5(9): 466–74.

Stammler, F. (2005) 'The Obschina Movement in Yamal: Defending Territories to Build Identities?' in E. Kasten (ed.) *Rebuilding Identities. Pathways in Post-Soviet Siberia*, Berlin: Dietrich Reiner Verlag.

Stefansson, V. (1943) 'The Logic of the Air', *Fortune* 4 (April): 70–75.

Steinberg, P., Gerhardt, H. and Tasch, J. (2012) 'The Arctic Model', *Harvard International Review* (30 June), hir.harvard.edu/crafting-the-city/the-arctic-model?page=0,5.

Stern, P. (2010) *Daily Life of the Inuit*, Santa Barbara: Greenwood.

Stokke, O. and Honneland, G. (eds) (2007) *International Cooperation and Arctic Governance*, Abingdon, Oxfordshire: Routledge.

Store, J. and Lavrov, S. (2010) 'Joint Communiqué', *Globe & Mail* (Canada) (21 September).

Sweden Government (2011) *Sweden's Strategy for the Arctic Region*, Stockholm.

Taagholt, J. and Hansen, J. (2001) *Greenland: Security Perspectives*, trans. Daniel Lufkin, Fairbanks, Alaska: Arctic Research Consortium of the United States.

Tenenbaum, D. (2004) 'POPs in Polar Bears: Organochlorines Affect Bone Density', *Environmental Health Perspectives* 112(17): A1011.

UIA (2009) *Union of International Associations database*, www.uia.be (accessed 12 May 2009).

Umbreit, A. (2009) *Spitsbergen, Svalbard, Franz Joseph Land, Jan Mayen*, 4th edition, Chalfont St Peter, UK: Bradt Travel Guides.

UNEP (2009) *POPs*, www.chem.unep.ch/pops/ (accessed 7 July 2009).

UNEP and International Eco-Tourism Society (2007) *Tourism in the Polar Regions. The Sustainability Challenge.*

US Government (2009) *Homeland Security Directive on Arctic Regional Policy*, Washington.

USGS (2008) *Survey of Undiscovered Oil and Gas in the Arctic*, US Geological Society.

Usher, M.B. (with Callaghan, T.V., Gilchrist, G., Heal, B., Juday, G.P., Loeng, H., Muir, M.A.K. and Prestrud, P.) (2010) 'Human Impacts on the

Biodiversity of the Arctic', *Encyclopedia of the Earth*, www.eoearth.org/article/Human_impacts_on_the_biodiversity_of_the_Arctic (accessed 15 December 2010).

Van Miegham, J. and Landsberg, E. (1958) *Advances in Geophysics*, Vol. 5, London and New York: Academic Press.

Waltz, K. (1979) *Theory of International Politics*, Reading, MA: Addison-Wesley.

Watt-Cloutier, S., Fenge, T. and Crowley, P. (2005) 'Responding to Climate Change: The View of the Inuit Circumpolar Conference on the Arctic Climate Impact Assessment', in L. Rosentrater (ed.) *2° is Too Much! Evidence and Implications of Dangerous Climate Change in the Arctic*, Oslo: WWF International Arctic Programme, 57–70.

Webb, T. (2010) 'Cairn Energy Fails to Find Enough Oil off the Coast of Greenland', *Guardian* 26 October.

Wegge, N. (2011) 'The Political Order in the Arctic: Power Structures, Regimes and Influence', *Polar Record* 47(241): 165–76.

Weir, D. and Schapiro, M. (1981) *Circle of Poison*, San Francisco: Institute for Food and Development Policy.

Wessendorf, K. (2011) *The Indigenous World 2011*, Copenhagen: International Work Group for Indigenous Affairs.

White, P. (2010) 'TB Once Again Stalking the Arctic', *Globe & Mail* (12 December).

WikiLeaks (2010) 'Canadian PM and NATO S-G Discuss Afghanistan, the Strategic Concept and the Arctic', cable no. 244500, 20 January, 6.49pm, US Embassy Ottawa.

Wille, C., Kutzbach, L., Sachs, T., Wagner, D. and Pfeiffer, E.-M. (2008) 'Methane Emission from Siberian Arctic Polygonal Tundra: Eddy Covariance Measurements and Modelling', *Global Change Biology* 14: 1385–408.

Windeyer, C. (2010) 'ICC Leader: Greenland Moving Too Fast into Oil and Gas', NunatsiaqOnline, 11 May, www.nunatsiaqonline.ca/stories/article/9876_icc_leader_greenland_moving_too_fast_into_oil_and_gas/.

Wrenn, S. (1978) 'First Inuit Circumpolar Conference', *Polar Record* 19(118): 64–66.

WWF (2010) *Drilling for Oil in the Arctic: Too Soon, too Risky*, Geneva: WWF.

Young, O. (1985) 'The Age of the Arctic', *Foreign Policy* 61: 160–79.

——(2002) 'Can the Arctic Council and Northern Forum Find Common Ground?' *Polar Record* 38(207): 289–96.

——(2011a) 'If an Arctic Ocean Treaty is not the Solution, What is the Alternative?' *Polar Record* 47(4): 327–34.

——(2011b) 'The Future of the Arctic: Cauldron of Conflict or Zone of Peace? (Review Article)', *International Affairs* 87(1): 185–93.

Young, O. and Osherenko, G. (1993) *Polar Politics*, Ithaca, NY: Cornell University Press.

Zeeberg, J. (2001) *Climate and Glacial History of the Novaya Zemlya Archipelago, Russian Arctic*, Amsterdam: Rozenberg.

Zellen, B. (2010) 'Clan, the State and War, Lessons from the Far North', *Joint Force Quarterly* 58 (July).

Ziker, J. (2002) 'Land Use and Economic Change Among the Dolgan and the Nganasan', in E. Kasten (ed.) *People and the Land: Pathways to Reform in Post-soviet Siberia*, Berlin: Lynne Reimer, 191–208.

Index

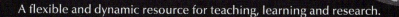